THE VOICE OF
THE CHURCH
A FORUM ON LITURGICAL TRANSLATION

THE VOICE OF THE CHURCH
A FORUM ON LITURGICAL TRANSLATION

Ad Hoc Committee on the Forum on the Principles of Translation
National Conference of Catholic Bishops

With Contributions by Gilbert Ostdiek, Jeremy Driscoll,
Stanislaus Campbell, and Dennis D. McManus

United States Catholic Conference • Washington, D.C.

The Voice of the Church assembles the papers delivered at the NCCB-sponsored symposium on liturgical translation held November 26-27, 1998. The Ad Hoc Committee on the Forum on the Principles of Liturgical Translation, which organized and directed that event, was chaired by Archbishop Jerome G. Hanus, OSB, who approved the final editing of these papers. Their publication is authorized by the undersigned.

Monsignor William P. Fay
General Secretary
NCCB/USCC

Cover: *St. Jerome Reading* by Georges de La Tour (1593-1652). Louvre, Paris, France. Réunion des Musées Nationaux/Art Resource, N.Y.

First Printing, June 2001

ISBN 1-57455-427-1

Like a caring mother, the Church, through the teaching of Vatican Council II, has called on its children, in full awareness of their responsibility in the Body of Christ, to share actively in the liturgical prayers and rites. For this reason, the Church has permitted the translation of texts venerable for their antiquity, devotion, beauty, and long-standing use. That is proof of the exalted duty and weighty responsibilities of those who translate such texts. The translations published here and there prior to the promulgation of the Constitution on the Liturgy had as their purpose to assist the faithful's understanding of the rite celebrated in Latin; they were aids to people untrained in this ancient language. The translations now, however, have become part of the rites themselves; they have become the voice of the Church.

—Paul VI, Address to Translators of Liturgical Texts
November 10, 1965

CONTENTS

GENESIS

ARCHBISHOP JEROME G. HANUS, OSB

In June 1994 the National Conference of Catholic Bishops (NCCB) sponsored a two-day workshop for member bishops on the translation of liturgical texts from Latin into English. Held during the summer meeting of the Conference in La Jolla, California, the workshop was moderated by Dennis D. McManus, then patristics editor for the Ancient Christian Writers Series of Paulist Press and an adjunct professor of theology at Drew University. The title of his address, later published in the *BCL Newsletter* (vol. 30 [June/July 1994]: 166-171), was "Principles of Translation: Issues in the Application of the Hermeneutics of *Comme le prévoit*." It was on that occasion that Dennis McManus asked, "Could it be time for the Conference to consider the creation of a forum which can help to address the host of issues surrounding vernacularization in those areas of church life continually affected by them?"

In response to his suggestion, the November 1994 plenary assembly of the NCCB approved the formation of an ad hoc committee to design a scholarly forum on issues involved in the translation only of liturgical texts. Subsequently, Archbishop William Keeler, then president of the NCCB/ USCC, named Archbishop Jerome G. Hanus, OSB, as chair of the Ad Hoc Committee on the Forum on the Principles of

Translation, whose other members would include Archbishop Justin Rigali, Archbishop Alexander Brunett, Bishop Victor Balke, and Bishop Joseph Gerry, OSB.

While concerns about the translation of other ecclesiastical texts such as the *Catechism of the Catholic Church*, the Scriptures, the *Code of Canon Law*, and magisterial statements had arisen in the years immediately previous, the Conference assigned only those issues associated with the translation of liturgical texts as the province of the ad hoc committee. During the process of obtaining the required *recognitio* for the revised translation of the *Lectionary for Mass* and the Sacramentary (Roman Missal), specific issues associated with the translation of liturgical texts had come to the fore. As a result, the ad hoc committee identified the following five principal tasks in the design of the Forum itself: (1) to locate experts and staff who could be invited by the Conference president as presenters and participants at the Forum, (2) to find other interested parties whose insights on vernacularization could be of benefit to participants, (3) to determine the manner of invitation to the Forum for bishop members and others, (4) to set a date and place for the Forum, and (5) to establish the practical details of the Forum program.

At the Conference's June 1995 plenary session, Archbishop Hanus presented an initial design for the Forum, which included the following goals for presenters and participants: (1) to increase awareness and appreciation of what the

Church has taught in its various documents on translation of sacred, especially liturgical, texts; (2) to clarify the nature of Latin as a sacred language and to identify the special claims this nature makes on vernacularization; (3) to review what has been accomplished in the English-speaking world through thirty years of translation since Vatican Council II; (4) to develop appropriate hermeneutics especially for liturgical vernacularization; (5) to suggest revision in the hermeneutics of vernacularization as appropriate; (6) to promote greater informed awareness, charity, ecclesial and pastoral sensitivity, and respect for the universal nature of the Church in future discussions on liturgical translation; (7) to encourage a greater consistency in the translation of all ecclesiastical texts so that fewer differences in the language of worship, law, catechetics, and teaching might be evident for the faithful; and (8) to increase an understanding of the theological and cultural contexts in which the task of vernacularization takes place. By a vote of 127 to 66, the Conference gave approval to the president to authorize the production of the Forum as designed by the ad hoc committee. At the same meeting, the NCCB approved funding to cover the Forum's sponsorship of participants and publication of materials.

With the succession of Bishop Anthony M. Pilla as president of the NCCB/USCC in November 1995, the Ad Hoc Committee on the Forum on the Principles of Translation was reappointed with its original members, now staffed by Sr. Ann Rehrauer, OSF, associate director of the Secretariat for the Liturgy. Dennis McManus was then invited by the ad hoc committee to serve as moderator of the Forum. In addition, six presenters, seventeen bishops, and three non-Conference member guests were invited as participants. Every member bishop of the NCCB was invited to attend.

Originally, the Forum was scheduled to take place in June 1997 immediately following the NCCB meeting in Kansas City, Missouri. However, several events in late 1996 and early 1997 caused the ad hoc committee to reconsider this date. Chief among these was the receipt of a June 13, 1996, announcement that Archbishop Geraldo Majello Agnelo, archbishop-secretary of the Congregation for Divine Worship and the Discipline of the Sacraments, addressed to the ICEL (International Commission on English in the Liturgy) Episcopal Board: *Comme le prévoit* did indeed contain valuable principles of liturgical translation, but it was in need of review. Some months later, the Congregation released a February 1, 1997, letter from Cardinal Angelo Sodano, secretary of state, directing Archbishop Arturo Medina-Estevez, prefect of the Congregation, to develop a new document on the translation of liturgical texts. In addition, the Conference and two Roman congregations—Doctrine of the Faith, as well as Divine Worship and the Discipline of the Sacraments—held considerable discussions and exchanged several documents in connection with the revision of the *Lectionary for Mass*.

On May 6, 1997, Archbishop Hanus met with Sr. Ann Rehrauer, Dennis McManus, and several consultants to discuss the wisdom of postponing the Forum in light of these developments. Several of the scheduled presenters expressed grave doubts about being able to make presentations in the wake of the Holy See's announcement on the intended revision of *Comme le prévoit*, especially if the anticipated new document were not to be made available to the presenters in a timely manner. As a result of these concerns, Archbishop Hanus and the members of the ad hoc committee decided to postpone the Forum and to prepare a new design for its participants and observers that would try to incorporate the results of ongoing consultation with others on the nature of liturgical translation, as well as information from the Holy See on the anticipated successor document to *Comme le prévoit*.

In the meantime, Dennis McManus was hired as a second associate director for the Secretariat for the Liturgy at the NCCB and was asked to work with Sr. Ann Rehrauer and to continue serving as moderator of the Forum. By August 1998, a revised proposal for the structure of the Forum was presented to the ad hoc committee. With committee approval, Dennis McManus and Sr. Ann Rehrauer then set out to organize a two-day symposium that would include thirty-five participants: three scholar-presenters, seventeen member bishops of the NCCB, two representatives of the Congregation for Divine Worship and the Discipline of the Sacraments, five other NCCB staff members, and five additional guests, including the directorship of the secretariat of ICEL in Washington, D.C.

The full list of participants and attendees is given below.

PARTICIPANTS AND ATTENDEES
AT THE FORUM ON TRANSLATION

Bishop-Participants
1. Cardinal Francis George, OMI
2. Bishop Joseph A. Fiorenza, President, NCCB/USCC
3. Archbishop Jerome G. Hanus, OSB
4. Archbishop Daniel E. Pilarczyk
5. Archbishop Justin F. Rigali
6. Archbishop William J. Levada
7. Archbishop Elden F. Curtiss
8. Bishop William K. Weigand
9. Bishop Patrick R. Cooney
10. Bishop Joseph J. Gerry
11. Bishop John J. Myers
12. Bishop Alfred C. Hughes
13. Bishop Thomas G. Doran
14. Bishop Richard J. Sklba
15. Bishop Emil A. Wcela

Bishop Observers
16. Bishop Daniel P. Reilly
17. Bishop Allen H. Vigneron
18. Bishop Blase J. Cupich

Representatives from the
Congregation for Divine Worship
19. Abbot Cuthbert Johnson, OSB
20. Rev. Michael Magee

NCCB Staff Members

21. Msgr. Dennis M. Schnurr
22. Msgr. William P. Fay
23. Sr. Sharon Euart, RSM
24. Rev. James Moroney
25. Sr. Ann Rehrauer, OSF
26. Mr. Dennis D. McManus

ICEL Secretariat

27. Dr. John Page
28. Mr. Peter Finn

Observers

29. Bishop Raymond Lahey
30. Sr. Rosa Maria Icaza, CCVI
31. Msgr. Francis Mannion
32. Rev. Kevin Irwin

Presenters

33. Rev. Gilbert Ostdiek, OFM
34. Rev. Jeremy Driscoll, OSB
35. Br. Stanislaus Campbell, FSC

The revised design of the Forum included two goals: (1) the presentation of differing views on liturgical translation, and (2) the development of a common process for addressing the translation issues identified. The purpose of the revised Forum did not include the identification of solutions to the problems themselves, but rather the development of processes that might assist in finding solutions. During the course of the two-day discussions, methodological issues in translation were to be given special focus. The Ad Hoc Committee on the Forum on the Principles of Translation hoped that some level of consensus might emerge among the bishop-participants regarding how translation issues should be treated within the NCCB.

The Forum on Translation was convoked on November 19, 1998, immediately following the previous week's plenary session of the NCCB. Forum sessions were held at the NCCB headquarters in Washington, D.C., and were concluded on the afternoon of November 20, 1998. Below are the three principal speakers chosen to give papers on issues in liturgical translation:

- **Rev. Gilbert Ostdiek, OFM,** *Professor of Liturgy and Theology at the Catholic Theological Union in Chicago, Illinois.* His paper, entitled "Liturgical Translation: Some Reflections," addressed the nature of liturgical prayer from the experience of those who make up the worshiping assembly. Fr. Ostdiek approached his topic through an examination of prayer in its liturgical texts, the contexts of liturgical prayer, inculturation, and finally, liturgical translation.

- **Rev. Jeremy Driscoll, OSB,** *Professor of Monastic Studies and Liturgy at Mt. Angel Abbey, Oregon, and at San Anselmo, Rome.* In his paper, "Conceiving the Translating Task: The Roman Missal and the Vernacular," Fr. Driscoll proposed five points for consideration: (1) his conception of the task of translating a patristic text; (2) the possible applications of such a conception to translation of the Roman Missal; (3) the broad issues and perspectives that a successful translator of the Roman Missal ought to identify and adopt; (4) examples from the 1997 ICEL translation of the Roman Missal that raise reservations in light of the previous point; and (5) suggestions about the spiritual dimensions of the translating task.

- **Br. Stanislaus Campbell, FSC,** *Auxiliary Provincial of the District of San Francisco of the Brothers of the Christian Schools.* Br. Campbell delivered an address entitled "Pastoral Issues in the Translation of Liturgical Texts." In it, he addressed six principal points: (1) translated texts draw all those engaged in liturgy to an active participation that is as full as possible; (2) translated texts respect the narrative form of liturgical prayer; (3) translated texts are appropriately metaphoric; (4) translated texts incorporate inclusive language; (5) translated texts are substantial enough for repeated use as prayer over a lengthy period of time; and (6) translated texts respect the principle of "organic growth" advocated by the Second Vatican Council itself (cf. *Sacrosanctum Concilium* [*Constitution on the Sacred Liturgy*], no. 23).

Each presentation was followed by an intense period of questions and answers that principally, though not exclusively, engaged the author in a clarification, defense, or development of his thesis.

The second half of the program, reserved mostly for November 20, found all participants in a general discussion not only of how the three addresses converged and differed in theoretical points and practical application, but also of what principles of translation should be used in connection with liturgical books.

The three presenters were once again invited to offer reflections on their papers in light of the intervening discussions held by the entire group. Dennis McManus facilitated a closing discussion among all the participants on the nature of liturgical translation.

This present publication concludes the work of the Ad Hoc Committee on the Forum on the Principles of Translation.

WELCOMING
REMARKS

It is a great pleasure to welcome all of you to this symposium on the issues which face the National Conference of Catholic Bishops (NCCB) in the translation of liturgical texts. With some eighteen bishop-participants, two observers from the Congregation for Divine Worship and the Discipline of the Sacraments, eight scholars, and several staff from the NCCB General and Liturgy Secretariats, we are a diverse group of pastors, academics, and administrators who share the Conciliar vision to promote a liturgy which facilitates the enjoyment of "full, conscious and active participation in liturgical celebrations" (*Sacrosanctum Concilium* [SC], no. 14). And surely it is in that same spirit that the Council itself decreed that the reform of liturgical books should incorporate vernacular language which incorporates "legitimate variations and adaptations to different groups, regions and peoples" (SC, no. 38), while sustaining the substantial unity of the Roman Rite.

It is in connection with this second task that the Consilium for the Implementation of the Liturgy issued its January 1969 instruction *Comme le prévoit* as a first reflection on how the vernacularization of liturgical texts should take its direction. Numerous other, less-known instructions on the translation of Latin liturgical texts into the vernacular then followed. Such documents as *Circa Instructionem* (March 1969) and *Plures Liturgicae* (September 1969), dealing with *ad interim* translation and the translation of new liturgical texts, respectively, began to extend and apply the directives of *Comme le prévoit* to a variety of translation challenges which the post-Conciliar commission faced. By 1980, the Holy See had issued eighteen separate documents regulating the translation and publication of liturgical books into vernacular languages.

Since then, and with the rising interest in "inculturation" as an aspect of liturgical studies, the Holy See and national episcopal conferences have grown ever more sensitive to the way in which liturgical language legitimately incorporates diverse elements of local culture into the worship of the Church. Chief among these is the use of vernacular languages, both in translation of the Latin texts in the Roman Missal and in composition of original texts foreseen by the 1969 statement of the Consilium, *Comme le prévoit* (cf. 43), and further outlined in the 1994 instruction by the Congregation for Divine Worship and the Discipline of the Sacraments, *Varietates Legitimae* (cf. nos. 53, 54-62).

At the same time, it must be stated that the use and adaptation of the vernacular within the liturgy has been paralleled by the use of the vernacular in biblical and catechetical translations. Indeed, our own experience as a Conference clearly suggests that what we have learned from the translation of non-liturgical texts such as the *Catechism* has had a direct effect on our understanding of how to render biblical Greek and Hebrew as well as ecclesiastical and liturgical Latin.

It would be an understatement to observe that difficulties in the translation of biblical, catechetical, and liturgical texts had become, by the summer of this year (1998), the single most time-consuming issue facing the Conference. In the last four years, the Conference has devoted more time to the discussion and approval of the Lectionary, Sacramentary, and other liturgical texts than to almost any other category of business. Additionally, the NCCB has sponsored for its own members three separate workshops since 1994 on the problems faced in the translation of liturgical books in particular.

It was following one such study day held in La Jolla, California, in June of 1994, that then-Archbishop William Keeler, as president of the NCCB, established an ad hoc committee to address translation issues in greater depth relative to liturgy. After the November 1995 meeting of the Conference, Bishop Anthony M. Pilla, then president, appointed me as chairman of a new committee charged with arranging a symposium or forum to consider translation issues in the liturgy. He also asked Archbishop Justin Rigali, Archbishop Alexander Brunett, Bishop Victor Balke, and Bishop Joseph Gerry, OSB, to accept committee membership. Sr. Ann Rehrauer, OSF, was appointed secretary to the committee.

During the next two years, the ad hoc committee researched and prepared a list of suggested participants for the Forum, including bishops and linguistic and translation scholars. These participants were then invited to attend by Bishop Pilla, and the Forum was scheduled to be held in Washington in June 1997. However, in the course of the special process to prepare the final revisions to the *Lectionary for Mass* in March 1997, it became apparent that any discussion on the translation of liturgical texts would have to reflect and incorporate the experience gained by the working group for the final revisions of the *Lectionary*. For that reason, a decision was made to postpone the Forum originally scheduled for June 1997 and to prepare a Forum with a modified format for November 1998 immediately following the NCCB meeting. Since that time, further issues regarding liturgical translations have arisen with the texts for the rite of ordination.

Mr. Dennis D. McManus, the moderator of the Forum, joined the Liturgy Secretariat staff in October 1997. With advice from a small committee of scholars and translation experts, he prepared a new format for the Forum which we will enjoy over the next two days.

As a final note, I would like to welcome individually our three invited speakers, Fr. Gil Ostdiek, OFM, Fr. Jeremy Driscoll, OSB, and Br. Stanislaus Campbell, FSC, each a proven scholar and liturgist whose insights we seek on the issues at hand. As well, we are pleased to host Abbot Cuthbert Johnson, OSB, of the Benedictine Abbey of Quarr, on the Isle of Wight, Great Britain, and the Rev. Michael Magee, who together represent the Congregation for Divine Worship and the Discipline of the Sacraments.

It is the hope of the ad hoc committee of the bishops' conference that this Forum on Translation will assist not only our own country but the entire Church to appreciate and to begin to find answers to the many issues of vernacularization which the renewal of the liturgy from the Second Vatican Council has invited us to explore.

† Most Rev. Jerome G. Hanus, OSB
Chairman, Ad Hoc Committee on the Forum
on the Principles of Translation

Thank you, Archbishop Hanus, for your kind remarks. As president of the National Conference of Catholic Bishops, I am very pleased to welcome each of you to our headquarters here in Washington for your two-day symposium addressing issues in liturgical translation. The Bishops' Ad Hoc Committee on the Forum, under Archbishop Hanus's able direction, has prepared an excellent program which asks for your attention in the vitally important area of the translation of liturgical texts.

Yours will not be an easy task. For the last five years, the bishops have struggled very publicly and honestly with the proposed translation of the Sacramentary. And for the last twelve years, we have labored hard to produce a new translation of the *Lectionary for Mass*, the first volume of which we are proud to see will be available for use in just another week or so with the start of Advent. The tasks which you have set for yourselves in these two days—to identify the issues we face as a Conference in the translation of liturgical texts, and to suggest a process whereby these issues might be addressed—can be of immense service to the bishops. I look forward to seeing the results of your work.

It is a pleasure also to acknowledge the presence of so distinguished a group of scholars, especially the three guest speakers—Fr. Gil Ostdiek, OFM; Fr. Jeremy Driscoll, OSB; and Br. Stanislaus Campbell, FSC—who will address you today.

I know that we as bishops are heartened by the supportive presence of Abbot Cuthbert Johnson, OSB, and Fr. Michael Magee as representatives of His Eminence, Cardinal Medina, Prefect of the Congregation for Divine Worship and the Discipline of the Sacraments.

Be assured of my prayers for the success of your undertaking. I commend you to the intercession of St. Jerome, the great translator of the Vulgate, who knew well the difficulties you face.

Thank you.

† Most Rev. Joseph A. Fiorenza
President, NCCB/USCC

LITURGICAL TRANSLATION: SOME REFLECTIONS

GILBERT OSTDIEK, OFM

Introduction

It is an honor for me (and no little cause for apprehension) to speak today on an issue that has claimed so much attention of late and occasioned more than a little difference of opinion and even divisiveness in our Church. I was invited to take part in this forum because of my association with the translation work of ICEL (International Commission on English in the Liturgy) for more than a decade. In accepting the invitation it was clear to me, however, that I was not being asked to speak officially in the name of ICEL. What I say today has without doubt been influenced by those years at ICEL. But there has been an even more significant influence. As a member of the liturgical assembly I owe a far greater debt to the extraordinary grace and privilege that has been ours in these decades since Vatican II, the grace of participating fully, consciously, and actively in the renewed liturgy, offering God our prayer and praise in our own tongue. The convictions I bring to what I say about liturgical translation are rooted most deeply in that experience.

In the fall of 1965, Pope Paul VI addressed liturgical translators assembled in Rome for a conference on their new task.
Translations into the vernacular, he told them, "have become
part of the rites themselves; they have become the voice of
the Church" gathered in prayer (in DOL,[1] no. 787). They
now serve a different purpose, he said, for they are no longer
merely aids to understanding for those untrained in Latin.

---

1 The following abbreviations are used in this article:

- DOL   ICEL, *Documents on the Liturgy, 1963-1979: Conciliar, Papal, and Curial Texts*, ed.
  and trans. Thomas C. O'Brien (Collegeville, Minn.: Liturgical Press, 1982).
  References are to marginal numbers.

- **Vatican II constitutions and decrees**
  AG   *Ad Gentes* (*Decree on the Church's Missionary Activity*), 1965.
  DV   *Dei Verbum* (*Dogmatic Constitution on Divine Revelation*), 1965.
  GS   *Gaudium et Spes* (*Pastoral Constitution on the Church in the Modern World*), 1965.
  SC   *Sacrosanctum Concilium* (*Constitution on the Sacred Liturgy*), 1963.

  All can be found in Austin Flannery, ed., *Vatican Council II: The Concilar and Post
  Conciliar Documents*, vol. 1, new rev. ed. (Northport, N.Y.: Costello Publishing, 1996).

- **Other papal and curial documents**
  CT   John Paul II, *Catechesi Tradendae* (*On Catechesis in Our Time*), 1979 (Washington,
  D.C.: United States Catholic Conference, 1979).
  EN   Paul VI, *Evangelii Nuntiandi* (*On Evangelization in the Modern World*), 1975
  (Washington, D.C.: United States Catholic Conference, 1975).
  GDC   Congregation for the Clergy, *General Directory for Catechesis*, 1997 (Washington,
  D.C.: United States Catholic Conference, 1998).
  IRL   *Inculturation and the Roman Liturgy* (usually cited as *Varietates Legitimae*), 1994
  (Washington, D.C.: United States Catholic Conference, 1994).
  RM   John Paul II, *Redemptoris Missio* (*On the Permanent Validity of the Church's
  Missionary Mandate*), 1990 (Washington, D.C.: United States Catholic
  Conference, 1991).
  TLT   *Instruction: Translation of Liturgical Texts* (often cited as *Comme le prévoit*), 1969, in
  DOL, nos. 838-880. Cited herein by internal paragraph numbers.

That time had passed. Letting go of our Latin heritage, however, was not easily done. On March 7, 1965, the day the use of the vernacular went into effect, Paul VI told those assembled for the Angelus in St. Peter's Square:

> The Church has sacrificed its native tongue, Latin, a language that is sacred, measured, beautiful, richly expressive, and graceful. The Church has made the sacrifice of an age-old tradition and above all of unity in language among diverse peoples to bow to a higher universality, an outreach to all peoples. (in DOL, no. 399)

What we and all peoples have gained through that resolute pastoral action initiated by Vatican II is slowly bearing fruit. In these past decades our assemblies have truly become the *ecclesia orans*. And that has been a grace indeed.

But three decades are only a brief moment in our tradition. It ought not surprise us that our efforts at crafting English words that truly "pray and sing" have not always been as successful as one might have hoped. After all, it has been a millennium and a half since we last undertook vernacularization in the late fourth century, when Latin came to be adopted in Rome through the efforts of North Africa.[2] The art of shaping prayer texts in the vernacular has to be learned anew and constantly honed, even as our newly minted English texts are

---

2   On the role of North Africa, cf. Anscar Chupungco, "The Cultural and Domestic Tradition of the Eucharist," in his *Worship: Progress and Tradition* (Beltsville, Md.: The Pastoral Press, 1995), 25-30.

quickly brought into our Sunday assemblies to become our prayer. And so it is appropriate now, after these few years, to pause and ask how we might do better.

The task assigned to me is not to explain or defend ICEL's approach to translation, but to focus on the larger issues facing us in the light of that experience. In the time allotted to me I will reflect on four areas: prayer texts, contexts, inculturation, and liturgical translation. (These areas are not airtight; you will note some overlapping.) In each area I will name clusters of issues as I see them, exploring their various dimensions and sketching some possible agenda items we might consider in order to carry out more fully the Vatican II renewal of the liturgy. I offer these reflections, in hope, as one liturgical theologian's contribution to furthering that dialogue.

Issues and Agenda

Issue One: Prayer Texts

Three facets seem important here: the translated texts of the liturgy are first and foremost prayer; they are the prayer of the assembly gathered here and now; and they are proclaimed and heard.

First, to repeat the words of Paul VI quoted earlier, liturgical translations now become the "voice of the Church." Important as classical considerations of *ecclesia docens* and *ecclesia discens* may be when we approach liturgy as a *locus theologicus*, we must never forget that the texts proclaimed in the assembly must become the living prayer of the *ecclesia orans*,[3] just as musical scores come alive in a concert and scripts on the theater stage. Prayer texts are primarily doxological and only secondarily didactic.[4]

The issue, then, is this: What makes a text come alive as a prayer? What makes a text memorable?[5] In a culture such as ours, we have learned to turn off our ears to the words that bombard us; we listen selectively. What is there about an effective prayer that engages the religious imagination of the hearers, that invites us to dwell in it and respond to it in faith? Certainly it has something to do with imagery—evocative images, especially biblical images, that connect the great biblical stories with our life experience and give us a glimpse

---

3 Glossing those words of Paul VI, TLT, no. 6, says: "The purpose of liturgical translations is to proclaim the message of salvation to believers and to express the prayer of the Church to the Lord."

4 Cf. the SCDW circular letter of April 27, 1973, *Eucharistiae Participationem*, no. 8: "The character of the eucharistic prayer that must have precedence therefore is that it is a giving of thanks for the entire mystery of salvation or for some feature of that mystery being celebrated in the liturgy according to the different days, feasts, seasons, or rites. Its catechetical character, directed toward bringing out the special features of a particular celebration, is secondary." In DOL, no. 1982.

5 Compare the following texts for their memorability.

Easter VII—Alternate Opening Prayer
Eternal Father,
reaching from end to end of the universe,
and ordering all things with your mighty arm:
for you, time is the unfolding of truth that already is,
the unveiling of beauty that is yet to be. (*continued*)

of God's hand still at work among us today, as in the previous generations of our people, to heal us and make us holy. It also has something to do with the beauty, the oral rhythm and flow, the very sound of the words—all those qualities of powerful language summed up in the word "stylistics."[6] And above all it has to do with words that leave behind a memory trace—e.g., "Fourscore and seven years ago . . ." and "a death he freely accepted . . ."—a memory trace that can readily be retrieved and evoked when the assembly gathers again. Truly prayerful texts communicate more than understanding for the mind; they evoke affect in the heart, resolve in our will, and a sense of being swept up into the story of salvation being

---

Easter VII—Alternate Opening Prayer (*continued*)
Your Son has saved us in history
by rising from the dead,
so that transcending time he might free us from death.
May his presence among us
lead to the vision of unlimited truth
and unfold the beauty of your love.
We ask this in the name of Jesus the Lord.

Preface IV for Weekdays
You have no need of our praise,
yet our desire to thank you is itself your gift.
Our prayer of thanksgiving adds nothing to your greatness,
but makes us grow in your grace,
through Jesus Christ our Lord.

(Texts taken from *The Sacramentary* [Washington, D.C.: ICEL, 1997]. This translation has not yet been affirmed by the Holy See.)

6   Cf. H. G. Widdowson, *Practical Stylistics* (New York: Oxford University Press, 1992).

proclaimed, into the return of praise and thanks being offered in the assembly. They embed themselves in our Christian consciousness, always ready to well up.

An agenda intent on studying this issue further might well take its cue from *Instruction IV: Inculturation and the Roman Liturgy*, no. 30, where we read:

> To prepare an inculturation of the liturgy, episcopal conferences should call upon people who are competent both in the liturgical tradition of the Roman rite and in the appreciation of local cultural values. Preliminary studies of a historical, anthropological, exegetical and theological character are necessary. But these need to be examined in the light of the pastoral experience of the local clergy, especially those born in the country. The advice of "wise people" of the country, whose human wisdom is enriched by the light of the Gospel, would also be valuable.

Note that the conversation partners for the work of preparing liturgical texts to be presented to the conferences include not only historians, exegetes, and theologians, whose voices are already represented around the translation worktable. Social scientists also have a role to play. What help can they provide us in understanding how prayers are crafted and function?

Might there not be insights to be gained from current studies on verbal learning, on cognitive processes and the meta-phoric structure of the human brain, on the physiology of hearing, on the human imagination, on synesthesia?[7] These disciplines have taken our understanding of human communication and knowing well beyond the scholastic axioms we learned as philosophy students: *"quidquid recipitur . . ."* and *"nihil in intellectu nisi prius in sensu."* These studies explore in detail the sensory and physiological basis of how our inner human processes of knowing and communication occur. They are an untapped resource. The conversation partners named up to this point can be engaged through an extension of the kinds of background research already in place in the preparation of translations. But according to the fourth instruction (*Varietates Legitimae*), another set of partners is to be included in the process of preparing inculturated texts. These include experienced local clergy and those who are "wise" in the ways of both the Gospel and their culture. ICEL now uses preparatory consultations to gather the experience

---

7   Sample references would include the following: Irving Massey, "Words and Images: Harmony and Dissonance," *Georgia Review* 34 (1980): 375ff; Allan Paivio, *Imagery and Verbal Processes* (New York: Holt, Rinehart and Winston, 1971); John Foley, "An Aural Basis for Oral Liturgical Prayer," *Worship* 56 (1982): 132-152; Eva T. H. Brann, *The World of the Imagination: Sum and Substance* (Lanham, Md.: Rowman & Littlefield, 1991); Mark Johnson, *The Body in the Mind: The Bodily Basis of Meaning, Imagination, and Reason* (Chicago: University of Chicago Press, 1987); Richard E. Cytowic, *Synesthesia: A Union of the Senses* (New York: Springer-Verlag, 1989). For more on metaphor and liturgy, see *Liturgy Digest* 4:1 (1997).

and wisdom of this group of folks. Should field studies of their experience be undertaken in a more systematic way?[8] What more might be done to engage them in the actual work of preparing effective prayer texts? Are there ways to extend their involvement in the process? How can we ensure that their voices are heard as we translate, revise, and review texts? Might it not be possible to enlist their collaboration in testing out our proposed translations in actual liturgical celebrations, with proper authorization, before the texts are presented to the conferences for response and eventual approval?

Second, liturgical prayer is to be the prayer of the assembly. "In [the liturgy] the whole public worship is performed by the Mystical Body of Jesus Christ, that is, by the Head and his members" (SC, no. 7). In our liturgical tradition, the public prayers of the Church are typically cast in the first-person plural and are to evoke the "Amen" of those present. This

---

8   A quiet development is taking place in a new field that Mark Searle has called "pastoral liturgical studies." See his "New Tasks, New Methods: The Emergence of Pastoral Liturgical Studies," *Worship* 57 (1983): 291-308. Drawing on social science methodologies, this approach to the study of liturgy collects data through the techniques of participant observation at actual celebrations, interprets the meaning of that data, and critically compares these findings and interpretations with what liturgical history and theology have to say about the meaning of the rite. For further comment on the theory and practice of this approach, see several articles by Margaret Mary Kelleher: "Hermeneutics in the Study of Liturgical Performance," *Worship* 67 (1993): 292-318; "Liturgical Theology: A Task and a Method," *Worship* 62 (1988): 2-25; "Liturgy: An Ecclesial Act of Meaning," *Worship* 59 (1985): 482-497; and "Ritual Studies and the Eucharist: Paying Attention to Performance," in Martin Connell, ed., *Eucharist: Toward the Third Millennium* (Chicago: Liturgy Training Publications, 1977), 51-64.

means that the assembly called to prayer is not hypothetical or abstract; it is an actual assembly gathered here and now. The implication is clear: "The formula translated must become the genuine prayer of the congregation and in it each of its members should be able to find or express himself or herself" (TLT, no. 20). Further, there is a commissive quality to liturgical prayer; in answering, "Amen," the assembly commits itself to a way of life that embodies gospel values of love, service, reconciliation, and justice.

The issue, then, is whether the prayers speak to this assembled people, draw them into prayer in God's presence, and evoke their faith and their Christian commitment to live as disciples sent into today's world. What kind of language do we need for that? A parallel might be drawn with what the Church has said regarding evangelization:

> The individual Churches . . . have the task of assimilating the essence of the Gospel message and of transposing it, without the slightest betrayal of its essential truth, into the language that these particular people understand, then of proclaiming it in this language.

> The transposition has to be done with the discernment, seriousness, respect and competence which the matter calls for in the field of liturgical expression, and in the areas of catechesis, theological formulation, secondary ecclesial structures, and ministries. And the word "language" should be understood here less in the

semantic or literary sense than in the sense which one may call anthropological and cultural.

The question is undoubtedly a delicate one. Evangelization loses much of its force and effectiveness if it does not take into consideration the actual people to whom it is addressed, if it does not use their language, their signs and symbols, if it does not answer the questions they ask, and if it does not have an impact on their concrete life. (EN, no. 63)

That last sentence applies equally well to the "field of liturgical expression." Such expression also "loses much of its force and effectiveness if it does not take into consideration the actual people to whom it is addressed, if it does not use their language, their signs and symbols, if it does not answer the questions they ask, and if it does not have an impact on their concrete life." And note the insistence that it be the living language of this particular people. But lest we think that no limits are placed on translation, the text continues:

But on the other hand evangelization risks losing its power and disappearing altogether if one empties or adulterates its content under the pretext of translating it; if, in other words, one sacrifices this reality and destroys the unity without which there is no universality, out of a wish to adapt a universal reality to a local situation. Now, only a Church which preserves the awareness of her universality and shows that she is in fact universal is capable of having a message which can be heard by all, regardless of regional frontiers. (EN, no. 63)

Stress on the living language of each particular people has implications for our agenda for the future. We will need to attend more fully to the narrative power of our prayers, especially as we move more heavily into multicultural parish life.[9] How do people of a particular culture identify the story of God's saving deeds in their own lives? What prayer forms and kinds of language are most apt to lead people to sense this and acknowledge it in wonder, praise, and petition? How is that story modulated in cross-cultural contexts to gather up unique human experiences into the Christian master story enshrined in the life of our Lord? To what extent must its message and linguistic forms be richly multivalent in multicultural communities?

Third, the liturgy's prayers are proclaimed and heard; they are by their very nature oral/aural. A text that is stored in print or electronic media to be retrieved later is one thing; words shaped to be spoken and heard are another. One may well wonder whether in assessing translated prayers we tend to pay too much attention to a text in its written form, asking questions about fidelity and precision, and too little attention to its suitability for oral proclamation and hearing.

---

9   Semiotics and narrative theory can be of help here. Cf., for example, Kathleen Hughes, *The Language of Liturgy: Some Theoretical and Practical Implications* (An ICEL Occasional Paper) (Washington, D.C.: ICEL, n. d.).

Let me draw this out a little more. Those who work in the field of humanities and anthropology tell us that text is an "inscribing medium," while utterance/speech is an "incorporating medium." For written prayer texts to be effective, they have to approximate speech/utterance. The more they do, the easier it is for a presider to lift them off the page and bring them to life for the assembly. Walter Ong has studied the difference between what he calls "primary oral cultures" and "literate cultures."[10] Oral cultures know nothing of writing or of reducing words to sign residues which can be stored and retrieved later; words are always spoken, sounded, power-laden. Think of the Hebrew understanding of God's word, *dabar*. Word not only says—it does what it says, it is event. In contrast to literate cultures, oral cultures show a predilection for a different style of speech. The contrasts noted by Ong include the following:

- For understanding and retention, oral style relies on rhythmic, balanced patterns, on repetition and antithesis, on alliteration and assonance; literate style relies on the ability to go back and re-read the inscribed text.

- Oral style prefers to join ideas with conjunctions; literate style opts for subordinate clauses.

---

10 Walter Ong, *Orality and Literacy: The Technologizing of the Word* (New York: Methuen, 1982), esp. chapter three: "Some Psychodynamics of Orality."

- Oral style uses parallels, contrasts, epithets to keep things related; literate style separates and analyzes them.

- Oral style seeks redundance and is richly layered; literate style avoids redundance and is more spare.

- Oral style speaks concretely of actual situations; literate style favors abstraction.

According to anthropologists, the words of ritual function more in the way speech does in oral cultures. This also serves the corporate purposes of ritual, for oral/aural language has a characteristic capacity to hold a group together (literally spell-bound) and to facilitate remembrance and reiteration. Understanding orality is essential to understanding ritual performance. We need to keep it on our agenda.

Another kind of question comes to mind in light of this. Has our liturgical language, like our worship space, become too plain and unadorned to feed the sacramental imagination of the faithful? Do teenagers have it right when they say, "Boring!"? Might not the language of the liturgical prayer be served better by the characteristics of orality than of literacy? The Roman rite in its fifth-century incarnation is said to be characterized by "noble simplicity," and this was put forward in Vatican II as the ideal for the liturgical renewal (cf. SC, no. 34).[11] The liturgical renewal has taken this ideal quite seriously both in unadorned architecture and in a spare style of English. Nevertheless, other periods in the history of the Latin rite and other historical Christian rites suggest that in other contexts liturgy thrives on repetition, formulaic phrases easily remembered, redundancy, concreteness, and life-relatedness in the language of prayer. Though the dominant North American culture cannot be said to retain a heavy residue of orality, the experience of many in our assemblies suggests that orality has much to offer in making prayers memorable and effective. The cultures of the British Isles, in contrast to the dominant culture in this country, still show the influence of orality. In particular, the Irish love of the graphic, vivid language of poetry, ballad, and song and the British love of the elegant flow of language have much to offer to balance our North American sense of blunt directness (resulting, most recently, in a growing governmental quest for "plain-speak" in its regulations). The great poetic and dramatic works of the Elizabethan period were written in an age when 90 percent of the people were said to be functionally illiterate. The works of Shakespeare, Milton, and Dryden, the King James Bible, and Cranmer's *Book of Common Prayer*

---

11 Cf. Mark Wedig, *The Hermeneutics of Religious Visual Art in l'Art Sacré 1945-1954 in the Context of Aesthetic Modernity* (Ph.D. dissertation, The Catholic University of America, 1995), 117-125. The author discusses the influence of the French Dominicans in establishing the current widespread adoption of a non-representational liturgical aesthetic. This aesthetic matches the ideal of the "noble simplicity" of the Roman liturgy as formulated by Edmund Bishop.

were all crafted to be heard. They are still effective bench-marks for spoken language today—not in their now-dated vocabulary and archaic idioms, but in their patterns of speech stresses, assonance, alliteration, and rhythmic flow. Would this not be a worthwhile area to explore in a future agenda dealing with liturgical translations that bring the riches of the English cultural heritage to the implanting of God's reign in our midst?[12]

Issue Two: Contexts

Again, there are several facets to this issue. In addition to their ritual context, the prayers are set within a complex symbol system and have multiple historical-cultural contexts.

First, prayers do not convey meaning as isolated verbal texts; they accompany and are set within ritual action. We have already alluded to the biblical understanding that word,

---

12 Cf. AG, no. 22. In this context, it is interesting to note what Pope Gregory the Great wrote to Augustine of Canterbury in A.D. 599/600, as recorded in Venerable Bede's *History of the English Church and People*, Bk. 1:27, trans. Leo Sherley-Price, rev. ed. (New York: Dorset Press, 1968), 73. Cf. also *Epistles of Gregory*, Book XI: Ep. LXIV, ad Q. 3, in *Nicene and Post-Nicene Fathers*, vol. 13:75 (Grand Rapids, Mich.: Eerdmans, 1956), 11. In an unpublished translation by Nathan Mitchell, the letter reads: "You know, brother, the custom of the Roman Church in which you were brought up; cherish it lovingly. But as far as I am concerned, if you've discovered something more pleasing to almighty God—in the Roman or the Gallican or any other church—choose carefully, gathering the best customs from many different churches, and arrange them for use in the church of the English, which is still a newcomer to the faith. For we should love things not because of the places where they're found, but because of the goodness they contain. Choose, therefore, those elements that are reverent (*pia*), devout (*religiosa*), and orthodox (*recta*), and gathering them all into a dish (as it were), place it on the table of the English as their customary diet."

dabar, enjoys the quality of deed as well. Vatican II spoke in a similar way about the complementarity and mutuality of word and deed:

> This economy of Revelation is realized by deeds and words, which are intrinsically bound up with each other. As a result, the works performed by God in the history of salvation show forth and bear out the doctrine and realities signified by the words; the words, for their part, proclaim the works, and bring to light the mystery they contain. (DV, no. 2)

This intrinsic connection between word and deed also holds true for the living tradition of the Church, particularly its sacramental worship.[13] To this we might add the biblical understanding of remembrance, *anamnesis*, which lies at the heart of liturgy as well. The euchological narration of God's saving deeds is not mere "psychological recall"; it has the quality of event.[14] In liturgy word and deed go hand in hand. The words work best when they name and embody the meaning of the rite and are in turn substantiated by it. This means that

---

13 For a fuller theological development of this connection, cf. Karl Rahner, "The Word and the Eucharist," in his *Theological Investigations IV* (Baltimore: Helicon, 1996), 253-286.

14 Cf. Bastiaan van Iersel, "Some Biblical Roots of the Christian Sacrament," in E. Schillebeeckx and Boniface Williams, eds., *The Sacraments in General: A New Perspective*, Concilium 31 (New York: Paulist, 1968), 5-20.

translators must be attentive to the relationship between the text and the liturgical action, aware of the needs of oral communication and sensitive to the literary qualities of the living language of the people. (IRL, no. 53)

Second, this can be expanded by noting that the words of liturgy are deeply woven into an interlocking web of other symbolic forms of communication—inflection and tone of voice, facial expression, gesture, posture, movement, space, and environment. Though the same prayer is proclaimed from celebration to celebration, the meaning it has in each celebration is subtly shaped by all that accompanies and surrounds it. Anthropology and linguistic studies, especially the field of semiotics,[15] now commonly hold that words do not have permanently fixed meaning regardless of context. Rather, their specific meaning is always contextualized, the result of the interplay of all the signs in the total system.

On both scores, the agenda for furthering the work of liturgical translation would be well served by an exploration of both the ritual context and the complex system of signs which form the larger field of discourse in which the translated texts are embedded. Contemporary anthropology and

---

15 For an introduction to this highly technical field, cf. Nathan Mitchell, "Lexicon," *Liturgy Digest* 2:1 (1994): 24-103; for more extended commentary, cf. also Winfried Nöth, *Handbook of Semiotics* (Bloomington, Ind.: University of Indiana Press, 1990).

linguistics can serve as useful guides for that exploration,[16] and in particular a branch of stylistics that deals explicitly with "discourse analysis."[17]

Third, discerning the meaning to be brought forward in translating a Latin text requires locating it in its original context. That is not always as easy as it sounds. In some cases a prayer can be dated to a certain author (e.g., Pope Gregory) and/or a specific historical context (e.g., the Opening Prayer of Sunday VIII in Ordinary Time, composed by Pope Vigilius in the winter of 537-538, when Rome was under siege and about to be ransacked[18]). Often, however, the prayer has passed through the hands of redactors of different times and historical-cultural contexts. Furthermore, the Latin rite is also noted for its use of the "mosaic" principle by which a compiler borrows ideas and phrases from many different sources and blends them into one new prayer. In a real sense, such redacted and blended prayers carry with them the vestiges of multiple contexts and fields of discourse through which they have passed. Speaking of evangelization, Pope John Paul II wrote:

---

16 For an example of how semiotics can be applied to prayer texts and to music in the liturgy, cf. Mark Searle, "*Fons Vitae*: A Case Study in the Use of Liturgy as a Theological Source," in Gerard Austin, ed., *Fountain of Life*, NPM Studies in Church Music and Liturgy (Washington, D.C.: The Pastoral Press, 1991), 217-242; Jan Michael Joncas, "Semiotics and the Analysis of Liturgical Music," *Liturgical Ministry* 3 (Fall 1994): 144-154.

17 Cf. Henry G. Widdowson, ed., *Discourse in Action* (New York: Oxford University Press, 1981).

18 For commentary on how this was brought to bear in revising the prayer, cf. Gilbert Ostdiek, "Crafting English Prayer Texts: The ICEL Revision of the Sacramentary," *Studia Liturgica* 26:1 (1996): 128-139.

The Gospel message cannot be purely and simply isolated from the culture in which it was first inserted (the Biblical world or, more concretely, the cultural milieu in which Jesus of Nazareth lived), nor, without serious loss, from the cultures in which it has already been expressed down the centuries. . . . (CT, no. 53)

The meaning of the prayer text is never found in a pure state, as though its essence could be extracted from its cultural embodiment(s). And often the text, set in a series of changing contexts in the course of history, has undergone successive transformations as it has made its way to us.

The issue for translators and those with responsibility of oversight is obvious. Which stage of meaning is to be taken as the authentic one? For example, the meaning of *mereor* in fourth- and fifth-century rhetoric differs significantly from the meaning it later acquired in early medieval soteriology. Or which aspect of accumulated meanings is to be given preference? In such semantically complex and culturally multiple fields of discourse, editorial choices have to be made. That runs the risk, however, of fixing the meaning too precisely or narrowly, with the possibility of "serious loss" of some aspects of multivalent meaning found in the tradition. On the positive side, this process of successive transformations also opens the way to a new enrichment and fresh vitality of ancient texts.

The Congregation for Divine Worship and the Discipline of the Sacraments hopes that each particular church, especially the young churches, will discover that the diversity of certain elements of liturgical celebrations can be a source of enrichment, while respecting the substantial unity of the Roman rite, the unity of the whole church and the integrity of the faith transmitted to the saints for all time (cf. Jude 3). (IRL, no. 70)

The way forward, then, might be to enlarge our working understanding of the liturgy as constituting a vast repertoire of prayer texts which collectively, rather than individually, proclaims the fullness of the faith to us.

Issue Three: Inculturation
Reflection on the previous issue has already led us into the issue of inculturation. Several comments should be added at this point.

First, the Vatican II decision to allow vernacular back into the liturgy after more than a millennium was rooted in this basic pastoral principle: "In the reform and promotion of the liturgy, this full and active participation by all the people is the aim to be considered above all else" (SC, no. 14). The point to be noted here is that, although the Council envisioned a modest use of the vernacular and had its eyes fixed on the pastoral goal of participation in the liturgy by the entire assembly, this decision was in fact a radical acceptance of what has come to be called "inculturation." Why is that so? The instruction on inculturation puts it this way: The living language of a people (*sermo vivus*) is a preeminent means (*praecipuum instrumentum*) of communication among them (cf. IRL, no. 39). Language lies at the very heart of a culture. The missionary endeavors of the Church have been quick to recognize and act on this:

> The missionary tradition of the church has always sought to evangelize people in their own language. . . . And this is right, as it is by the mother language, which conveys the mentality and the culture of a people, that one can reach the soul, mold it in the Christian spirit and allow [it] to share more deeply in the prayer of the church. (IRL, no. 28)

Producing this kind of formative translation, whether of the Gospel or of the prayer of the Church, is not always easy. Lamin Sanneh recounts instances of how Bible translations by missionaries, though grammatically correct, were not appropriated by a local church because the language was not an authentic expression of the living, spoken language of the locale.[19]

Second, what, then, is inculturation and how does it happen? In *Redemptoris Missio* Pope John Paul II writes:

---

19 Cf. Lamin Sanneh, *Translating the Message: The Missionary Impact on Culture* (Maryknoll, N.Y.: Orbis, 1989).

The process of the Church's insertion into peoples' cultures is a lengthy one. It is not a matter of purely external adaptation, for inculturation "means the intimate transformation of the authentic cultural values through their integration into Christianity and the insertion of Christianity in the various human cultures." The process is thus a profound and all-embracing one, which involves the Christian message and also the Church's reflection and practice. But this is a difficult process, for it must in no way compromise the distinctiveness and integrity of the Christian faith. (RM, no. 52)

Reflecting on this, the instruction *Inculturation of the Roman Liturgy* says:

On the one hand the penetration of the Gospel into a given sociocultural milieu "gives inner fruitfulness to the spiritual qualities and gifts proper to each people . . . strengthens these qualities, perfects them and restores them in Christ." On the other hand, the church assimilates these values, when they are compatible with the Gospel, "to deepen understanding of Christ's message and give it more effective expression in the liturgy and in the many different aspects of the life of the community of believers." This double movement in the work of inculturation thus expresses one of the component elements of the mystery of the incarnation. (IRL, no. 4; quotations in text are from GS, no. 58)

Several things in this statement should be underlined. The theological basis for inculturation is the mystery of the incarnation itself,[20] in which divinity and humanity are wed. Inculturation is a double movement, involving a gradual, dialogical process in which a culture is christianized and Christianity is incarnated in a culture, assimilating compatible values of the culture.[21] This mutual interplay between Christianity and the host culture has been the object of growing research in sociocultural historical studies and mission studies.[22] Studies such as these indicate that there is far more cultural residue in our current liturgy than we might have imagined. These studies are well worth adding to the list of areas to be explored as the work of liturgical translation continues.

Noting that this kind of process needs to take place slowly and gradually, "in such a way that it really is an expression of the community's Christian experience," *Redemptoris Missio* goes on to quote what Paul VI said in Kampala:

---

20 Cf., for example, AG, no. 10; CT, no. 53; GDC, no. 109.

21 For two perspectives on how the process unfolds, cf. Ary A. Roest Crollius, "What Is so New About Inculturation? A Concept and Its Implications," *Gregorianum* 59 (1978): 733-734, which identifies the stages as translation, assimilation, and transformation; and Anscar Chupungco, "Liturgy and Inculturation," in Chupungco, ed., *Handbook for Liturgical Studies*, vol. 2: *Fundamental Liturgy* (Collegeville, Minn.: Liturgical Press–Pueblo Book, 1998), 337-375, which identifies the alternate methods of creative assimilation and dynamic equivalence.

22 Cf., for example, Richard Fletcher, *The Barbarian Conversion from Paganism to Christianity* (New York: Henry Holt, 1998); James C. Russell, *The Germanization of Early Medieval Christianity: A Sociohistorical Approach to Religious Transformation* (New York: Oxford University Press, 1994).

It will require an incubation of the Christian "mystery" in the genius of your people in order that its native voice, more clearly and frankly, may then be raised harmoniously in the chorus of other voices in the universal Church. (RM, no. 54)

One hears in these words an echo of St. Paul's one-word definition of liturgy in 2 Corinthians 1:20: "It is through him that we address our Amen to God when we worship together." All peoples of the universal Church form the chorus. The metaphor of incubation also echoes the fresh insight voiced in Vatican II's *Dei Verbum*:

The Tradition that comes from the apostles makes progress in the Church, with the help of the Holy Spirit. There is a growth in insight into the realities and words that are being passed on. This comes about in various ways. It comes through the contemplation and study of believers who ponder these things in their hearts (cf. Lk 2:19 and 51). It comes from the intimate sense of spiritual realities which they experience. And it comes from the preaching of those who have received, along with their right of succession in the episcopate, the sure charism of truth. Thus, as the centuries go by, the Church is always advancing toward the plenitude of divine truth, until eventually the words of God are fulfilled in her. (DV, no. 8)

Third, this vision of a Spirit-led Church working in consort to understand and live the Gospel anew in every time and place suggests that our agenda for the future must also include the question of how best to secure the collaboration of all who have a role in the process of inculturation. Inculturation, John Paul II says,

> is a slow journey, which accompanies the whole of missionary life. It involves those working in the Church's mission *ad gentes*, the Christian communities as they develop, and the Bishops, who have the task of providing discernment and encouragement for its implementation. (RM, no. 52)

What structures and procedures might enable us to apply these words to the work of liturgical translation? And what might we learn from the *General Directory for Catechesis*? In that document, theological understanding of inculturation and pastoral process seem to be so well integrated.

Issue Four: Translation
The final issue I wish to touch on, under three aspects, is that of liturgical translation.

First, unlike translations of prose or poetry, the translation of prayer texts for use in the liturgy is unique in that liturgical language has its own special characteristics: It is deeply impregnated by the Bible; certain words current in Latin use (*memoria, sacramentum*) took on a new meaning in the Christian faith. Certain Christian expressions can be transmitted from one language to another, as has happened in the past, for example in the case of *ecclesia, evangelium, baptisma, eucharistia.* (IRL, no. 53)

Hallowed terms in our tradition's vocabulary cannot be summarily disregarded. Foremost on our agenda for the liturgy must be a companion catechesis which breaks open the meaning of these words in our prayer, but without interrupting that prayer or distracting people from it.

Second, there is, however, another consideration. Our work of liturgical translation has much to gain from attending to what anthropology and linguistics are telling us about language and how it functions. Words, they tell us, communicate meaning only as part of a larger language system. This entails several things. What is to be translated is not individual words, but "a system of relationships."[23] Nor can the *translatio*, the "bringing over" of meaning from source language to receptor language, take place purely on the grammatical level. Grammar and syntax are specific to each

---

23   Richard Howard, a translator, quoted in Robert Wechsler, *Performing Without a Stage: The Art of Literary Translation* (North Haven, Conn.: Catbird Press, 1998), 116.

language and are part of its surface structure. Translation, then, cannot be reduced to simply connecting similar elements of surface structure in the two languages; it must work on the level of deep structure as well, where the semantic relationships of the two languages can meet.[24] Accordingly, anthropology and language studies now take it as commonplace that authentic translation must work in great measure on the principle of dynamic equivalence.[25] Transliteration can leave prayers sounding foreign and inaccessible, and formal equivalency does not automatically safe-

---

24 There are two alternate ways of drawing out this same implication. One, presented briefly above, is that of the narrative or story being remembered and retold in the language of a host culture. The other, developed in the field of structural linguistics since Ferdinand de Saussure, is that language is an act of "world construction" that names and gives intelligible shape to the world(s) in which we live. In both cases, it is not enough for liturgy to invite the worshipers to re-enter the historical-cultural story/world of the source text. In addition, the translated text must bring that story/world into the story/world of the hearers, so that they can recognize God's word and action addressed to them in their lives here and now. Translations that favor a more literal restatement of the source text tend to stress a return to the other world(s); translations that favor a more free restatement tend to stress the contemporary world(s) in which the message is received.

25 Wechsler, in *Performing Without a Stage* (op cit.), makes the same case from his extensive experience as an editor in the world of literary translations. In this context, we might also note the conclusion of Willis Barnstone, *The Poetics of Translation: History, Theory, Practice* (New Haven, Conn.: Yale University Press, 1993), 261: "What is impossible, all linguists agree, is synonymy or identity between two languages." But how is the "equivalence" required in translation to be understood? The phrases "formal equivalence" and "dynamic equivalence" may be now too associated with adversarial positions to be useful. Barnstone suggests the idea of a continuum, with literal translation at one end and free translation at the other. Either can be pushed to an extreme, slavish word-for-word literalism on the one hand and free imitation or paraphrase on the other. Formal and dynamic equivalence seem to move away from the two extremes and closer toward the middle. Cf. Barnstone, 226-262.

guard fidelity.[26] And dynamic translations can slip over into undisciplined paraphrase. Some work has already been done on this issue of equivalence in the fields of Scripture and theology;[27] but much remains to be done in the field of liturgy.[28] It would seem important, then, not to force a premature choice between these two approaches. Rather, the liturgical renewal is still in its early stages, and time is needed for our experience to mature, with the help of continuing reflection on what works best in our liturgical language.

---

26 Thus, the retention of the word "person" in our trinitarian theology can in fact mask a tritheistic understanding of the Blessed Trinity. Cf. Karl Rahner, *The Trinity*, trans. Joseph Donceel (New York: Herder and Herder, 1970).

27 Willis Barnstone, in *The Poetics of Translation* (op cit.), uses biblical translation as his basic illustration. Lamin Sanneh, in *Translating the Message* (op cit.), deals more directly with translation of the Bible. Charles H. Kraft, in *Christianity in Culture: A Study in Dynamic Biblical Theologizing in Cross-Cultural Perspective* (Maryknoll, N.Y.: Orbis, 1979), focuses on theologizing in mission work. Among professional translators of the Bible, dynamic equivalence has taken as axiomatic in recent years. But see the recent discussion of "functional equivalence" as an alternative, in Cecil Hargreaves, *A Translator's Freedom: Modern English Bibles and Their Language* (Sheffield, United Kingdom: Sheffield Academic Press, 1993).

28 Introductory surveys can be found in the following: Hermann Schmidt, "Language and Its Function in Christian Worship," *Studia Liturgica* 8 (1971): 1-25; Anscar Chupungco, "The Translation of Liturgical Texts," in Chupungco, ed., *Handbook for Liturgical Studies*, vol. 1: *Introduction to the Liturgy* (Collegeville, Minn.: Liturgical Press, 1997), 381-397; and Renato de Zan, "Criticism and Interpretation of Liturgical Tests" and "Liturgical Textual Criticism," in ibid., 331-365 and 367-379. Cf. also Gail Ramshaw-Schmidt, *Christ in Sacred Speech: The Meaning of Liturgical Language* (Philadelphia: Fortress Press, 1986); and Anthony C. Thiselton, *Language, Liturgy and Meaning* (Bramcote, United Kingdom: Grove Books, 1974).

Third, Rome has directed that conferences sharing a common language share a common text.[29] It is essential that any agenda addressing the issues of liturgical translation be dealt with in an international manner. To neglect or withhold collaboration on that larger scale might have the unwanted effect of denying the gifts which small local Churches have to offer for the enrichment of all. From the other side, unilateral action by larger local Churches with more resources can result in a form of ecclesial colonialism. How can we address this issue of liturgical translation with mutuality and fitting Christian concern for other English-speaking local Churches? The model that comes to mind immediately is the translators' conference held in Rome in November 1965. Would it not be timely to reconvene such a gathering now? As on that earlier occasion, there would be much to gain if participants from the English-speaking world were to be joined by those from all the major modern languages.

Time permitting, I wish to add one more consideration to this last issue and, with your leave, to address it plainly. That is the issue of fidelity and infidelity in liturgical translation. Over the past several years we have all heard and read critical comments that have crossed the boundaries not only of civility, but of Christian charity. Some helpful insight into this question can be found in a book by Robert Wechsler, *Performing Without a Stage*. In a chapter entitled "The Romance of Infidelity," he notes that "fidelity" has taken on

---

29 See the policies and procedures set down for "mixed commissions" in TLT, nos. 38-42.

unexpected moral overtones. At the head of the chapter he says, "Fidelity is the basic ethical term in translation. Infidelity means a translator's betrayal of the original work and its author."[30] In a lengthy reflection on this profession, this author, who serves as translation editor for a publishing firm, wrestles with the question of why critics of a translator's work so quickly cross over into moral judgement of the translator. The book is well worth reading for that alone, and it has forced me to ask if we might not need to wrestle with that same question in our Church. The issue is less one of liturgical translation than of pastoral care. My fervent hope is that it will find its way onto our agenda for the future.

Conclusion

I began by quoting the words of Paul VI: that the vernacular is now the voice of the Church's prayer. I wish to end there by acknowledging that in approaching the four issues named above—liturgical texts as prayer, some contexts of that prayer, inculturation, and liturgical translation—I have consciously chosen to set my perspective from within the praying assembly. I realize that there are other important aspects that must not be neglected. I have chosen the assembly's viewpoint for two reasons. First, the *Constitution on the Sacred Liturgy* stresses the significative, communicative function of the liturgy (cf. SC, no. 7) and has directed, "In

---

30   Wechsler, *Performing Without a Stage*, op cit., 65.

this reform, both texts and rites should be so drawn up that they express more clearly the holy things they signify and that the Christian people, as far as possible, be able to understand them with ease . . ." (SC, no. 21). Communication is paramount. And second, it seems to me that the folks in the pew are the ones we too easily forget when debate over translations turns rancorous. In the end, serving the People of God in their prayer, so that they can truly join themselves with the Lord in offering thanks and praise, in offering themselves and making of their lives a "living sacrifice of praise"—that is our common cause. The hope I harbor is that through our efforts, the unity of our heritage will not only be preserved, but enriched again and again by what each particular Church, whether young or old, brings to the celebration of the liturgy (cf. IRL, no. 70).

CONCEIVING THE TRANSLATING TASK: THE ROMAN MISSAL AND THE VERNACULAR

JEREMY DRISCOLL, OSB

Introduction

I want to speak to you today about the question of translating the Roman Missal into a vernacular English from the perspectives that landed me this invitation to address you. As I understand it, I have been asked for two reasons. One is that a portion of my professional work as a theologian involves translating patristic texts into English. Another is that I served for three years as an advisor to the Bishops' Committee on the Liturgy during the time when the committee and the Conference as a whole were reviewing the proposed ICEL (International Commission on English in the Liturgy) translations of the Roman Missal. The question put to me by the organizers of this forum was simply what perspectives do I have on the task of translating the Missal given this background.

I propose organizing my reflections around five major points. First, I would like briefly to describe how I conceive the task as I set out to translate a patristic text. Second, I will ask how much of this might apply or not to translating the Roman Missal. Third, I will try to express what I think are the broad issues and perspectives that a successful translator of the Missal ought to identify and adopt. Fourth, on the basis of the foregoing, I will offer you some examples from the proposed translation that raise reservations in me. Finally, I will draw conclusions designed to provoke your further discussion and offer some images for considering the spiritual dimension of the translating task.

I. Translating Patristic Texts

When I take up a patristic text, I am keenly aware that I am entering another world, a world considerably different from my own. I must try to understand it as completely as possible, noting with as much detail as I can exactly where these differences lie. There are large theological frameworks underlying the text. I must be competent in these, understand them, and appreciate them.

That might be enough if I were only wanting to read the text for myself. But if the task is translation, then I must go on to identify the key vocabulary of this world that I am entering, noting especially how some words or groups of words carry a special burden in building up this world. Some words mean something within this world that may be slightly different from their meaning in the language as it is used outside of it. Behind the use of other words lie big stories: doctrinal controversies, experiences of the Church at large or of particular churches, important turning points in the history of the Christian community. As I try to build up a sensitivity to this vocabulary, I look for what could be called "echo words," that is, words which echo ideas and understandings expressed in other ways. Any world built up by words is full of nuance, connections, and associations. I try to become aware of as much of this as possible.

All this can be conceived as a preliminary preparation for the translator. When I undertake to translate a particular text, I must be conscious of and extremely sensitive to this larger "con-text." With such preparation I can undertake to translate the text itself. Here my first step is to be certain that I understand it exactly. This takes a number of passes, for I am a foreigner in this world; and I do not catch it all the first time through. If I am not humble and even nervous about my foreign status, I might think I have understood it all when in fact my understanding is only partial. My goal of "understanding exactly" will include appreciating the way in which whatever is expressed has been rendered in the particular genius of that language. There is also a tone, a feeling, to the whole. This too is a part of what must be understood, for it is not a naked content that I am translating but a whole world of thought and feeling which are inextricably intertwined. As I work on understanding a particular text, I will note carefully the vocabulary, marking for special attention those words which carry the burden or those words which are meant to echo something not explicitly said.

So far I am describing only what I must do to understand the text. Then I try to translate *all* that I have understood. I employ, of course, my own language's genius to do so; and for this I need a set of sensitivities that parallel my sensitivities to the foreign tongue. But if I am skilled in my own language— or let me speak more energetically—if I am in love with it and what it can do, then I will not be afraid to let the original language suggest new possibilities in mine, pushing it to places it may not go on its own initiative. In any case, I am committed to using every conceivable device to get three things right: the content, the tone, and the special vocabulary. We could call all this a searching for the inner text, or the inner voice of the text. It is why translation is called an art. Like any art, it comes together in the end through intuition and creativity, but these are of little use to the artist who has not first been prepared in a thorough knowledge of and skill with the materials being dealt with.[1]

---

1   I have been helped in my own conceiving of the task by an essay of the fine American poet and translator Robert Bly: cf. "The Eight Stages of Translation," in *Translation: Literary, Linguistic, and Philosophical Perspectives,* ed. William Frawley (Newark: University of Delaware Press, 1984), 67-89. Though not all the stages that Bly identifies are relevant, I am especially helped by the fifth stage, which he calls "getting the tone right"; cf. 77-81: "We need the ear again, not the ear turned outward toward human speech, but the ear turned inward toward the complicated feelings the poem is carrying. Each poem has a mood." Kathleen Norris might also be cited as another American poet and writer with sensitivities to tone, and she comments directly on liturgical and biblical translations in at least two places: cf. *The Cloister Walk* (New York: Riverhead Books, 1996), 154-158; and *The Psalms,* the King James Version with commentary by Norris (New York: Riverhead Books, 1997), v-xxiii.

I study patristics and translate texts from this period because they are *not* like my world. It is their difference that I am interested in. But then (lo!) at some point I discover that this *difference* is relevant to my present, for it frees me from my narrow and unexamined perspectives. I could not discover this relevance had I not translated the difference.

II. How This Could Apply to Translating the Roman Missal

What of this process might be useful in conceiving the task of translating the Roman Missal? I see first some immediate differences.

In patristics, history and difference have the greater weight and should control and inspire the translation. One is dealing with a text that is written and read, the product of a single author. In liturgy, on the other hand, one is translating a text to be used in contemporary worship, and to some extent history and difference create a gap that needs to be bridged. The text is oral and proclaimed, not written and read; and it is the product not of one author but is an eclectic text produced during centuries. At the very least, this complicates the task.

Nonetheless, some of what I said about translating patristics might prove helpful also here. For example, with the Roman

Missal a whole world is being entered, and it is different from—or at least more than—my own mundane and everyday world. It is bigger than my own understanding of the Christian faith or of my particular community's understanding of that faith, even of my own culture's understanding. This bigger world has a vocabulary with a history that expresses it and builds it up. There are echo words which echo huge understandings of the mystery we celebrate. And so in undertaking the translation of particular texts of the Missal, I would be inclined to conceive the task in a way somewhat similar to how I described patristic translation.

That is, I first make sure I understand the text exactly in its own language. This includes, as I have said, appreciating the particular genius with which that language has expressed something. It likewise includes detecting the tone or feeling of the whole. I will want to note particular vocabulary, the words which carry special burdens and those that echo other dimensions of the liturgy not explicitly expressed in the particular text I am setting out to translate. It is, in short, a search for the inner text or the inner voice of the text.

III. What Are the Translating Issues in the Roman Missal?

I have spoken of a whole world into which the translator enters—of special vocabulary, echoes, tones, and feelings. Let me try to be more concrete now as I attempt to identify what

I think some of these are in the Roman Missal and thus what somehow has to be translated.

The liturgy is a mysterious world in the technical theological sense of the term. As tradition has it—and this from Scripture itself—"mystery" is a label for concrete "somethings" within which a divine reality is concealed. In the encounter with the mystery, with the concrete something, the divine reality is in part revealed and participated in. And thus the term "mystery" came to describe not only the material means of the revelation but also the otherwise imperceptible divine realities.[2]

Christology instructs us that the Lord's earthly life was itself a mystery: that is, a concrete something in which divine reality is concealed. "None of the rulers of this age knew the mystery. If they had, they would never have crucified the Lord of glory" (1 Cor 2:8; my translation). Thus we speak of

---

2 In teaching my students about these things, I have coined a phrase which I think fairly summarizes much of the patristic usage around the term "mystery." Founding the birth of the liturgy in the mystery of the Lord's Ascension, I say, "Today, what was history passes into mystery." The inspiration for this is an Ascension homily of Leo the Great, where he says, "*Quod itaque Redemptoris nostri conspicuum fuit, in sacramenta transivit. . . .*" Leo was explaining to his congregation that with the Lord's disappearance from our sight, all that he had done for us in his earthly existence was not finished but was now passing over into a new mode of being present to us: namely, in all the dimensions of the liturgy, that is, in mystery. Cf. Leo Sermon 74: 2, *Corpus Christianorum Latinorum* (CCL) 138A, 457. For the relation between *sacramentum* and *myterium* in the Latin tradition, cf. Y. Congar, "Le 'mysterion' applique aux sacrements, traduit par 'sacramentum' dans l'eglise ancienne" in *Un peuple messianique* (Paris: Cerf, 1974), 47-55. For an extended theological discussion of what I have condensed very simply here, see Louis Bouyer, *The Christian Mystery*, (Edinburgh: T & T Clark, 1989), especially 5-18, 131-171.

the mystery of his Nativity, of his Incarnation, of his death, his resurrection, and so forth. And we also name "mystery" the ultimate divine reality which all these dimensions of the Lord's life reveal: the mystery of the Holy Trinity.

This is the different world into which I enter when I enter the liturgy: a mysterious world. Every piece of the liturgy— language included—builds up this mysterious world and reveals divine realities, realities in themselves not directly perceivable by the senses. If I am going to translate the Roman Missal, then I need to be aware that its language at every turn touches up against these mysteries. Indeed, its language is itself a mystery: that is, a concrete something which mediates contact with divine realities.

Thus, everything in the liturgy is referential, referring to something which refers to something which refers to something which refers ultimately to the Holy Trinity and our participation in this divine communion. There is a huge coherence—a *Logos* (!)—which pervades it all. Every struc- ture and every mini-structure within the structures, every little *logos*, refers to the divine *Logos*, the divine coherence, which pervades it all and which has become flesh here. For our present purposes, thinking about translation, we must try to name and identify as many of these structures as possible. They can be thought of as large frameworks or patterns. Or we might want to call them a theological "syntax," meaning syntax not yet in the sense of language, but calling it that so that the connection with language will be more immediately evident. Syntax—the way in which things are put together and are held together—the particular genius of a particular tradition's expression.

In the Roman liturgy some of these frameworks or patterns— or call it "syntax"—would be the following: time and eternity, heaven and earth held together in a gratuitous communion; an anthropology of fallen and redeemed humanity; the past and future made present; salvation history present in mystery; the paschal sacrifice rendered present; the manifestation of and participation in the trinitarian mystery; the transformation of space and time in the *Hodie* of the feast; communion in holy things, that is, communion with other particular churches across the world and across time; communion with the saints in heaven and with the angels; the consequences of mission. A deep theological capacity is required to recognize and appreciate this world. It would not be sufficient for a translator to know Latin well and to have achieved a personal theological synthesis. The translator must be able to recognize exactly how and where Latin's use in this Missal expresses a specific theological vision larger than a personal synthesis is likely to be.

Coming more directly to the question of language from out of this vision of its larger context, we can observe that in the Roman Missal a particular vocabulary and syntax build up and continually refer to all these large themes that I have tried to identify. What is needed in translation is a vernacular equivalent of this particular vocabulary, a vernacular equivalent of the syntax, a vernacular equivalent of the coherence that allows constant reference and cross-reference, permitting the mysteries to echo off of each other.

We are not without guides in such an effort. The manner in which the Roman Missal accomplishes this can instruct us, for its language and vocabulary are scriptural and patristic. What "scriptural" means is obvious enough; but the translator must catch every citation, every phrase, every allusion—for the deepest meaning of the text to be translated relies on all that is contained in the scriptural passages alluded to.

To describe the Missal's language as patristic is a little more complicated, and yet a summary analysis of the dynamic of language in this period can suggest much about the translating task. First we should observe that the language of the patristic church was built up with particular meanings during the earliest and most formative period of the Christian tradition, one that has remained normative for the Church ever since.[3] The patristic tradition, to a large extent, is a particular way of reading Scripture. The Fathers wanted their language to be scriptural; they required this of themselves. And yet in

---

3   In *Dei Verbum* (*Dogmatic Constitution on Divine Revelation*), the Second Vatican Council has restated this normative status of patristics in nos. 8 and 11. For a detailed analysis of how this patristic norm works together with Scripture, cf. Cardinal Joseph Ratzinger, "Importance of the Fathers for the Structure of Faith," in his *Principles of Catholic Theology: Building Stones for a Fundamental Theology*, trans. Mary Frances McCarthy (San Francisco: Ignatius Press, 1987), 133-152.

a culture different from that which gave rise to the scriptural texts, such a requirement was not easily fulfilled. The Rule of Faith—a brief, somewhat fluid, verbal summary of the faith that came from the apostles—was an operative principle alive in all the churches. With this principle the Canon of Scripture and an orthodox way of reading it were determined. This Rule, intimately related to the profession of faith at baptism in the name of the Trinity, is likewise the basis for the more fixed summaries of the Creeds of the Councils and other conciliar formulae. But it is a principle which is through-and-through scriptural: it derives from Scripture, is its summary, and is used in turn to read it.[4]

It is only in this context of Scripture and the Rule of Faith that we can adequately understand the liturgy and how language is used there; for Scripture's most basic meaning is determined by the reality (the mystery!) accomplished in its proclamation in the liturgical assembly. What this reality and mystery are is fixed with precision by the language of the Rule of Faith, for Scripture just by itself can mean too many things, as the early Church's experience with gnosticism is sufficient to show. This liturgical context also indicates something crucial about the nature of the language of the Rule of Faith

---

4   For more on the Rule of Faith and Scripture, cf. James L. Kugel and Rowan A. Greer, *Early Biblical Interpretation* (Philadelphia: Westminster Press, 1986), 109-199. For the relation between baptismal creeds and the creeds of the Councils, cf. J. N. D. Kelly, *Early Christian Creeds* (London: Longman, 1972).

and the conciliar Creeds and doctrinal formulations which derive from it: namely, that the foundation for the content of faith lies in the mysterious realities achieved in the believing assembly wherein that faith is professed and celebrated. Thus we find that the "extra-scriptural" language of the patristic liturgies stands at an absolutely critical juncture between scriptural language and the more precise formulation of what the Church believes. What she believes is happening in the actual celebration of the liturgy. It is ultimately nothing less than communion in divine trinitarian life. Insofar as this is expressed in language, it is a very delicate interplay of scriptural, liturgical, and doctrinal language. In short, the language of the Roman Missal represents the synthesis of key ideas of biblical faith. This language is a *lex orandi* upon which a *lex credendi* is formulated. Of course, it could not be translated adequately unless the translator understands how this language is used. The christological, trinitarian, marian, ecclesial, anthropological, angelic realities and controversies and solutions are all reflected in the Missal's language; and they still matter for the Church today. All this must be translated.[5]

This last point about the scriptural and patristic language of the Missal and the need to translate precisely that has perhaps seemed complicated. Yet I believe that there is no

---

5   A model instrument, at least in regard to the Prefaces, in the hands of a translator who wants to be sensitive to the massive extent to which biblical and patristic language is employed in the Roman Missal is found in Anthony Ward and Cuthbert Johnson, *The Prefaces of the Roman Missal: A Source Compendium with Concordance and Indices* (Rome: Tipografia Poliglotta Vaticana, 1989). This work assembles the biblical and patristic texts cited or echoed in each of the Prefaces of the Roman Missal.

alternative but to understand the task in all its dimensions with their delicate interplay. There is but one further point to add as I try here to delineate the translating issues, taking cues from my experience as a translator of patristic texts. I have said it already in describing how I work in that field: namely, that a tone and feeling are created throughout the whole Missal as its language participates in the task of building up the mysterious world of the liturgy. This tone is distinctive to the Roman Missal, distinguishable from other great liturgical traditions in other languages. We do not have time to attempt a description of this tone, but the kind of adjectives for this which are generally employed can remind you of what I am speaking about. It is noble, sober, elegant, often restrained, but for that very reason sometimes notice-ably exuberant; it is reverent, precise, concise, admirable to hear, joyful, sorrowful, hopeful as the case requires. In trans-lating I try to re-create *this* tone in my language; and, as I said about translating patristics, I let this tone push my language in new directions. In my language I will have to employ rhetorical devices different from the original, but the goal is to create thereby the same tone.

IV. Examples of Problems in the Proposed Translation

I have sketched the issues here in broad strokes, as this is all that the short time available to us allows. Obviously my arguments need filling out and greater nuance. Nevertheless, I hope now that by examining some examples of what I consider problems in the proposed translation, at least my broad strokes will be secured enough to stimulate your further discussion. Here, too, of course, we are limited by the constraints of time; and so I feel it necessary to say at the outset that in my opinion the kinds of problems I will attempt to identify run right through the whole translation; and the effect is cumulative. In other words, maybe this or that particular text is not so bad or could be lived with, even admitting a problem. But if such problems were to be found in text after text, eventually the inner voice and the synthesis of faith which are to be translated will have slowly vanished. To be critical of the proposed translations is not for me or for many a question of turning back the reform of the liturgy, but indeed rather of wanting to confirm it and set it on secure ground.

I will treat these examples from the stage in the process that I have described as "understanding exactly," as opposed to offering alternative translations, which is a later step in the process. The various issues and dimensions that I identified one by one need now to be brought to bear symphonically in the examination of particular texts.

It will be useful to begin with a grammatical observation about conjunctions, and I am thinking especially about "*ut*," "*enim*," and "*quia*." Conjunctions in any language carry a large part of that language's capacity to express nuance and nuanced relations between otherwise separate ideas. A conjunction unites different parts of a sentence into a unique relation that could not exist were the different parts to stand as separate sentences. Furthermore, sometimes conjunctions are used in such a way as to cause different parts of an unfolding expression to "weigh" different amounts within the whole.

The Latin liturgical tradition exploits this capacity of conjunctions for, among other things, the expression of nuance in doctrine. Especially frequent in this regard is the use of "*ut*" with the beautiful subtlety of the subjunctive which as a rule follows it. I am speaking about compound and complex sentences which with their grammatical syntax express a theological syntax. ICEL has long argued that English cannot bear the same complexity of the Latin sentence structure, although in articulating principles for the revised translation, it did state "an openness to use a more complex English syntax."[6] I would have been much more thoroughgoing in my use of this. I think English bears it well, and so much of what the Latin accomplishes depends on it. Indeed, in English, just as in Latin, interest and attention are increased precisely because the hearer is waiting to hear what unfolds next. This effect is lost when the Latin is reduced to declarative statements standing side by side.[7]

---

6   Cf. in the ICEL archives, "Preliminary Comment and Principles: A Working Paper on the ICEL Revision of the Sacramentary, 1982-1994" (Draft), 15.

7   Anglicans have long successfully employed complex English sentences in their liturgical English, even retaining many of them, though simplified, in their revised liturgical books. Cf. Louis Weil, *Gathered to Pray: Understanding Liturgical Prayer* (Cambridge, Mass.: Cowley Publications, 1986), 87-122. Throughout this discussion Weil shows many examples of the use of complex sentences in the Anglican tradition. Thus it is odd that he himself says, on p. 103, "The complex relative clauses that characterize the Latin forms, and which Cranmer reshaped in the English versions, are not at home in modern English, whether spoken or written." Virtually everything else in the chapter indicates otherwise, including his own written sentences. Perhaps he felt required to repeat at some point what is so often said on the matter. But it is this that I want seriously to question.

With this and much of the rest of what I have already said in mind, let us attempt to "understand exactly" several texts. I do not presume that I will achieve such a goal, but the translator has to aim that high. In the Missal there are two Transfiguration Prefaces, one for the Second Sunday of Lent and the other for the feast itself. I want to focus on the text now, but as a translator I must require of myself an awareness of all that the mystery of Transfiguration means in the faith of the Church as well as an awareness of how this mystery will be made operative and revealed in the Eucharistic Prayer which begins at this point.

The theme of Transfiguration in the Lenten Preface echoes the gospel text for Mass on the second Sunday. This choice of readings is clearly designed to encourage the elect and to point their attention through the penance of Lent to the glory of the paschal sacraments which they will receive at Easter. The faithful accompany the elect in this journey. Those who hear this Preface, then, will have already heard the gospel text, with its language and images. They will also have heard, presumably, a homily on the text which further expounds such images and hopefully makes some connection between the text and the eucharistic sacrifice. Let us look now at just one complex sentence in this Preface and try to understand how it is meant to function in this "con-text."

We need not examine the standard opening (the protocol), apart from noticing that the *"per Christum Dominum nostrum"* with which it finishes is connected very tightly with what follows by the use of "*qui*." Perhaps a little unusual now in English to hold all that together with a "who," it still should be considered whether this connection is worth losing. In any case, it is wonderfully tight in the text I am trying to understand exactly:

LATIN	PROPOSED TRANSLATION[8]
. . . *per Christum Dominum nostrum.*	. . . through Jesus Christ our Lord.
Qui, propria morte praenuntiata discipulis,	Having told the disciples of his coming death
in monte sancto suam eis aperuit claritatem,	Jesus made his glory known to them on the holy mountain.
ut per passionem, etiam lege prophetisque testantibus,	With Moses and Elijah as witnesses,
ad gloriam resurrectionis perveniri constaret.	he revealed that the Christ had first to suffer
Et ideo. . . .	and so come to the glory of the resurrection.

What is the deep theological sense here? First of all, the one through whom we are now about to give thanks is the same one who in the past, having pre-announced his death, uncovered his glory on the mountain. This is already to say a great deal about the connection between the Gospel and the

---

8   The proposed translations provided throughout are taken from the 1997 ICEL *Sacramentary*, submitted for confirmation to the Holy See by the NCCB.

Eucharist we celebrate now. And he uncovered his glory for a specific purpose: to render firm what we might call a principle of the divine plan: namely, that one comes to the glory of the resurrection through the passion. This is tremendous! And therefore, "*et ideo*," we sing, "Holy, Holy, Holy," and offer the rest of the Eucharistic Prayer now.

So much is made to hold together here. In the proposed translation it does not seem to me to be as tight as it could be. To observe first the whole structure, the "*ut*" is not translated. Jesus' glorious manifestation is one sentence. The idea of glory through the Passion is another. But this connection is the very point of the Transfiguration. Christ uncovered his glory *so that* a precise something might be confirmed about something that is not glorious: namely, the Passion.

Let us look at some particular words and phrases. "*Praenuntio*"—a solemn word. Jesus is acting the prophet, like the Law and the prophets before him, who also foretold his death. The word reminds us of the phrase in 1 Peter 1:11 which speaks of the Spirit of Christ in the prophets as "*praenuntians eas quae in Christo sunt passiones et posteriores glorias.*" To say simply "Jesus told" for all this is insufficient.

"*Eis aperuit claritatem*"—a very definite verb, carrying the sense of uncovering, unveiling, exposing to view. To translate "Jesus made his glory known" is too intellective a rendering for the Transfiguration. There are a number of ways in which Jesus made his glory known (for example, changing water into wine, as in Jn 2:11). But here the logic is that of an unveiling to sight *in the body* of Jesus, the same body which is to undergo death. Leo the Great had used this word in a Lenten sermon on the Transfiguration where he wanted to stress very strongly the corporeal dimensions of the mystery: "*Aperit Dominus coram electis testibus gloriam suam, et communem illam cum ceteris corporis formam tanto splendore clarificat. . . .*"[9] This same verb is likewise found in a gospel text also clearly echoed in this Preface: "*Tunc aperuit illis sensum, ut intelliegerent Scripturas*" (Lk 24:44). So the unveiling of glory in his body is related to the unveiling of the meaning of the Law and the prophets.

"*Lege prophetisque testantibus*"—the proposal reads, "with Moses and Elijah as witnesses." This is odd; it might be described as an explanation in reverse. The listeners in this liturgy have already heard the gospel text and the homily explaining it. As liturgical texts often do, this Preface expresses the theological significance of the scriptural detail of the presence of Moses and Elijah, doing so with a phrase borrowed from elsewhere in the Scripture, still Luke 24. There is no reason to undo this in translation.

"*Ut per passionem . . . ad gloriam resurrectionis perveniri constaret*"—Here we are still clearly inside the logic of Luke 24 and the incredibly concise summary of the Law and prophets and the psalms that is expressed there by the risen Lord:

---

9   Sermon 51:3. CCL 138A, pp. 298-299.

namely, that the Christ had to suffer so to come to glory. These are expressions with which we are familiar, and they can be translated straightforwardly. But we should note the presence of a precise verb: "*consto.*" The proposal translates this as "revealed," but we saw that that idea had already been expressed with "*aperuit.*" Here the text expresses what the revelation was for. (It is governed by the "*ut.*") This verb has the sense of rendering firm, of establishing, almost of proving something. So to be precise, the revelation is not, as the proposal has it, that the Christ had first to suffer, etc. Rather, the revelation of glory in the body of Christ "proves" this principle.

This profound and condensed theological synthesis has expressed specific motives which inspire the assembly's thanksgiving in this moment. Latin expresses this with "*et ideo. . . .*" The proposed translation simply starts a new sentence. Granted, it is the next sentence to follow; the connection is weakened by failing to translate it. Surely, saying "and therefore" does not unduly complicate English syntax or strain listening capacities. And yet these several syllables accomplish a great deal theologically.

Finally, as we know, every Preface concludes with some way of expressing the communion of the assembly with the heavenly choirs. This Preface does so in a way particular to it and to the Preface used on the feast of the Transfiguration.[10] So, clue to the translator: There is something special here.

LATIN	PROPOSED TRANSLATION
Et ideo cum caelorum Virtutibus in terris te iugiter celebramus, maiestati tuae sine fine clamantes:	With joyful hearts we echo on earth the song of the angels in heaven as they praise your glory without end:

A specific choir of angels is singled out: "*virtutes*."[11] The word "*maiestas*" is used. ICEL almost always avoids translating this word as "majesty," perhaps with the argument that it carries connotations not suitable to contemporary mentality. However, a new vision of majesty is presented precisely by the

---

10 This same ending is also used for the following Prefaces: the Baptism of the Lord, the Annunciation, the Fifth Sunday of Lent (which refers to Lazarus), the Birth of the Baptist, the Preface for Martyrs, Christian Death V, and Preface II of the Blessed Virgin. These texts all have in common the mystery of the Lord's death or abasement and our share in the same.

11 Twenty-one Prefaces name the ranks of the angelic choirs, and these are never translated. What could justify this? The burden of the argument should lie with those who would want to leave these names out. Perhaps the suggestion would be advanced that people do not generally know of these ranks. But, of course, not naming them in the liturgy would be one of the principle reasons for this. For a shorthand reference on the importance, one could consult the *Catechism of the Catholic Church*, nos. 328-336.

The following are the problematic texts in this regard (page numbers refer to ICEL's Segment Four): Advent I, p. 2; Advent II, p. 2; Christmas I, p. 3; Lent I, p. 5; Lent IV, p. 7; Easter I, p. 13; Easter II, p. 13; Easter III, p. 14; Easter IV, p. 14; Easter V, p. 15; Ascension I, p. 15; Ascension II, p. 16; Pentecost, p. 17; Sunday Ordinary I, p. 18; Sunday Ordinary II, p. 18; Weekdays I, p. 23; Holy Cross, p. 27; Christ the King, p. 30; Blessed Virgin Mary I, p. 35; Joseph, Husband of Mary, p. 38; Christian Death I, p. 47. In short, this is a lot of instances of not mentioning the ranks of angels when the Latin liturgy does.

use of this word in these texts, all of which touch up against the mystery of the Passion. Thus does the word come to mean something in the liturgy that it may not mean elsewhere. Many words function in this way within the liturgy. In any case, there is no difficulty here with Latin. "*Maiestas*" in English is "majesty." The principal clause of this sentence is "*celebramus cum Virtutibus.*" Here the weight of the verb and action falls on the assembly, its celebrating on earth together with the Virtues of heaven. Perhaps the choice of the expression "'we echo' their praise," rather than "'we celebrate with' them," weakens the strength of the Church's song in this moment. In any case, the translator will ask questions like these, wanting to get the sense as exact as possible. Finally, the already exuberant verb "*celebrare*" is further strengthened by "*clamantes.*" We celebrate by crying out without end to your majesty. I do not hear the same tone and feeling in "With joyful hearts we echo."

I have spoken of the cumulative effects of the kinds of problems I am pointing out. What if this sort of loss should occur in text after text? To indicate this accumulation I choose as another example the other Preface of the Transfiguration so that we can rely on some of the foregoing observations and remain within the same basic mindset of the mystery.

LATIN	PROPOSED TRANSLATION
. . . *per Christum Dominum nostrum.*	. . . through Jesus Christ our Lord.
Qui coram electis testibus suam gloriam revelavit,	He revealed his glory before Peter, James, and John
et communem illam cum ceteris corporis formam	to strengthen his followers against the scandal of
maximo splendore perfuit,	the cross.
ut de cordibus discipulorum crucis scandalum tolleretur,	His human body shone like the sun
et in totius Ecclesiae corpore declararet implendum	to show that the whole Church, which is his Body,
quod eius mirabiliter praefulsit in capite.	will one day shine with the glory of Christ, its Head.
Et ideo. . . .	With joyful hearts we echo. . . .

To begin, I would apply a similar observation about the connective power of "*qui*." The one through whom we give thanks *now* is the same one whose transfiguration we now speak of in the *past* tense. "*Coram electis testibus,*" translated as "before Peter, James, and John," is once again an explanation in reverse. These names have been heard in the gospel text and in the homily. Now the liturgy expresses their theological significance: namely, that they are the elected witnesses without whose testimony we would know none of this. "*Coram*" is a strong and majestic preposition, most fitting to the extraordinary nature of the scene. The text gets some of its feel from this word, carrying a strong visual sense: in the presence of, before the eyes of, in the sight of. To say simply "before" is perhaps too weak to express this tone.

More serious is the observation of how the translators propose solving the admittedly complex phrases which circulate in a precise relationship around the word "*ut*." The proposed translation does attempt to show purpose (not with the expression "so that" but with the simple infinitive construc- tions "to strengthen" and "to show"). However, in an apparent attempt to simplify, the translation divides up the thoughts rather than connecting them. To speak first of the basic order of ideas, leaving an examination of specific vocabulary for later: the Lord did two things, revealed his glory and imbued his body with splendor. Both were done so that (*ut*) two other things could come about: the removal of the scandal of the cross and the revelation that the body of the Church will share the glory of her head. The English divides this up. It has it that the revelation of glory is to remove the scandal of the cross. Then the body imbued with splendor is to show something about the Church. But the theology expressed is considerably more powerful when the Latin order is preserved. What removes the scandal of the cross is not simply that the Lord revealed his glory but, more insistently, that he filled a body like ours with splendor. Likewise, it is not simply this latter that shows something about the whole Church, but the reve- lation of his glory before chosen witnesses.

If we examine the particular vocabulary with which this intricate pattern of ideas is expressed, we can see that a quite specific tone and feeling are created. There is an insistent pastoral point which the Latin makes with exuberance. It speaks of "*communem illam cum ceteris corporis formam maximo splendore perfudit.*" Every word here is beating home a point. "*Perfundo*" is an extremely vivid verb. Different from shining, it carries a sense of suffused, imbued, something pouring out of. The Lord suffuses not simply what is called his body but—lest the point be lost—that form of body which he shared in common with us. This common sharing is what removes the scandal of the cross and what declares the body of the Church related to the Lord's body. This body is suffused with total splendor. The strong expression—"splendor" is already a lot, but here it is "*maximo splendore*"—is meant to shock side by side with "a body like ours." The proposed "His human body shone like the sun" is a disappointing rendering of all this. It goes backwards into a mere citing of the biblical text, whereas the euchology expresses the deepened and digested significance of what the biblical text states. This language has been lifted word for word from Leo the Great's homily mentioned above, where the reasons for this doctrinal and pastoral insistence are further elaborated. In the total syntax of the liturgy, a homily like Leo's might have been preached this day. Leo's own text may have been heard in the Liturgy of the Hours.

The Latin has "*ut . . . crucis scandalum tolleretur,*" which carries the sense of taking away once and for all, removing forever, destroying. To say instead "to strengthen against the scandal" is weaker; it says less.

The translator's task becomes even more difficult in what follows, and what is proposed is good. Yet—I am still taking my cues from how I work personally as a translator of patristics—I feel uneasy, wondering if the complete feeling has been captured. I still taste in the text exuberance and insistence, a sense of wonder: "*ut . . . in totius Ecclesiae corpore declararet implendum quod eius mirabiliter praefulsit in capite.*" What language! Is "to show" sufficient for "*declaret*"? In Latin one feels the "*de-*" and the "*clar-*" and the achievement of "clar-ity." I want to try harder in my language for this feeling. And the grammatical form of "*implendum*" carries a definitive sense: that there is to be filled up in the body of the Church, which is stronger than the simple future which is proposed. And this verb "*praefulsit,*" a past tense contrasting with the future sense of "*implendum*"! One feels the "*prae-*"of this verb, shining outward from the body of the Lord in history to his body the Church. But there is no verb in the proposed translation to represent this past sense, and thus no contrast with the future. And somewhere in all this, to tack down this feeling with certainty, the Latin throws in a "*mirabiliter,*" and English can somehow say the same. Then the "*et ideo*" really has a reason for being there. Levels of wonder upon wonder bring us to celebrate by crying out with the Virtues of heaven!

Let us take a different kind of example now: one word, "*Unigenitus.*" In most instances in the proposed translation this word is rendered as "only Son." The effect of this, as opposed to the more expected "only-Begotten Son," should be carefully measured.[12] It is a word which occurs with noticeable frequency throughout Advent and the Christmas season, right through to Epiphany and the Baptism of the Lord, sounding again on the solemnities of St. Joseph and the Annunciation. Clearly there is some sort of connection among all the repeated uses of this title in prayers surrounding the mystery of the Lord's human birth. It is a clue to the translator to be sure in every instance to understand its significance within the seasonal pattern and to translate it in such a way that it echoes off the others. It would not be sufficient to argue, as some defenders of this proposal have done, that contemporary biblical translations—the term is of biblical origin—universally render it as "only Son." Very little is explained by this; for the biblical term, whose exact meaning was hotly contested in the theological disputes surrounding Nicea, comes to express for orthodox faith a precise position about the divine status of the Son, distinguishing his generation from that of creatures.[13] Thus, for the ear that can hear linguistic and theological echoes—and this must be the translator's ear—it should not

---

12 "*Unigenitus*" is a Christian neologism. With it Latin Christianity wanted to render with greater precision the Greek "*monogenes*." The Latin term becomes a technical term for the mystery of the unique filiation of Christ. Cf. René Braun, "Deus Christianorum," in *Recherches sur le vocabulaire doctrinal de Tertullien, second edition revue et augmentee* (Paris: Études Augustiniennes, 1977), 247-251.

13 In fact, concerning biblical translations, when the *Vetus Latina* translates the Greek "*monogenes*" either from the Septuagint (LXX) or the New Testament, it almost always says "*filius unicus*." However, by the time of the Vulgate a transition has been worked in theological Latin such that especially in the Johannine uses of the word (Jn 1:14, 18 and 3:16, 18; 1 Jn 4:9), which are the most critical for christology, it is always translated with "*Unigenitus*." Cf. Braun, op cit., 249, n. 3.

be possible to hear "*Unigenitus*" without hearing at the same time Nicea's insistence: "*genitum, non factum, consubstantialem Patri.*"[14] This is precisely the reason why the term occurs so frequently in prayers surrounding the Lord's human birth. It is a euchological expansion and digestion of the faith of Nicea and of the other christological and trinitarian developments which are based on Nicea.

Perhaps the most privileged biblical instance of this word is found in John 1:18: "*Deum nemo vidit unquam: unigenitus Filius, qui est in sinu Patris, ipse enarravit.*" For Nicean orthodoxy this verse, read as the climax of the whole Johannine prologue, speaks of the unique capacity of the Son—precisely because he is begotten, not made, consubstantial with the Father—to reveal the Father. It is a biblical term which has acquired a technical meaning. In all the prayers where it is used, it is meant to stress the Son in his divine eternal reality and then, either explicitly or by implication, throw into relief the contrast with his human birth. This is a syntax—a syntax to be translated.

I have found in an examination of Segment Two (Proper of Seasons) at least twenty-five instances where the term is not

---

14 At Nicea, the Greek "*monogenes,*" which is represented by "*Unigenitus*" in Latin, was acceptable to both Arians and the orthodox (of course, because it was a biblical term), but it was with the terms that followed it that a precise meaning was expressed for how "*monogenes*" was to be understood. Cf. Kelly's *Early Christian Creeds*, op cit., 234-254.

translated in this technical sense.[15] This would be another example of what I mean by cumulative effect. The Latin liturgy intends a different kind of cumulative effect: a season in which the word is heard again and again and thus acquires its meaning in the very context of the seasonal celebrations. The language of the Creed, which renders precise a biblical term, is filled out with the images of the feasts.[16]

One of the clearest examples of the doctrinal dimensions of the use of "*Unigenitus*" is found in the Opening Prayer on Monday in the weekdays of the Season of Christmas before the Epiphany of the Lord. In this prayer, the translators have clearly recognized the significance of the term and rendered it "only-begotten Son." The relevant phrase is "*qui Unigenitum tuum in tua tecum gloria sempiternum in veritate nostri corporis natum de Maria Virgine confitentur. . . .*" Here the contrast is clear between the "*Unigenitum*" and the "*natum de Maria.*" But this is meant to echo through the other prayers

15 The twenty-five instances are as follows: Opening Prayer (OP), Saturday First Advent; OP, Thursday Second Advent; OP, Friday Second Advent; OP, Saturday Second Advent; OP, Thursday Second Advent; OP, Friday Third Advent; OP, December 17; OP, December 18; OP, December 21; OP, December 25 Vigil; PAC, December 25 Vigil; OP, December 29; OP, December 30; Prayer Over the Gifts (POG), Sunday Second Christmas; OP, Thursday before Epiphany; OP, Epiphany; Prayer After Communion (PAC), Baptism of the Lord; OP, Wednesday 3rd Easter; POG, Presentation; POG, St. Joseph; POG, Annunciation; POG, Transfiguration; OP, Holy Cross; OP, Assumption Vigil Mass; PAC, November 2 II; OP, November 2 III.

16 The historical development of the liturgical celebration of Christmas unfolds together with the articulation of the christology and trinitarian implications of Nicea, Constantinople, Ephesus, and Chalcedon. This reaches a sort of climax in the Christmas preaching of St. Leo the Great and the euchology which relies on his language.

as well. For example, in another prayer in the phrase "*ut nos Unigeniti tui nova per carnem nativitas liberet,*" the theological syntax relies on the contrast between "*Unigenitus*" and something new: namely, his birth in the flesh. The proposed "grant that the birth of your only Son according to the flesh" misses this contrast.[17] Certainly orthodox faith is presumed for the interpretation of texts; nonetheless, translations should be as exact as possible when it is a question of doctrine. Grammatically this phrase can mean that Christ is the only Son according to the flesh. But *he* is the only Son by being the only-begotten Son, and this one has a *new* birth according to the flesh. Thus, a phrase like the following is required: "Grant that the new birth in the flesh of your only-begotten Son."

Another example is the phrase "*ut, qui . . . exspectata Unigeniti tui nova nativitate liberemur.*"[18] The same contrast occurs: a new nativity of the only-Begotten. The proposed translation says, "Grant that the birth of your only Son, so long awaited, yet always new. . . ." Again, grammatically this admits of no pre-existence for the Son, only the hope that a son be born. The "new" of the proposed translation is vaguely temporal; the "new" of the Latin is ontological.

The Advent and Christmas seasonal prayers again and again feel something startling: namely, that the eternal "*Unigenitus*"

---

17   This prayer occurs on December 30, Sixth Day in the Octave of Christmas.
18   OP, December 18.

should be born in time, in flesh. This contrast is always being drawn when the term is used. We hear it anew in the phrase *"ut, qui de Unigeniti tui in nostra carne adventu laetantur."* Simply translating "only Son" softens the contrast.[19] We hear the same contrast on the solemnity of St. Joseph: *"sicut beatus Ioseph Unigenito tuo, nato de Maria Virgine, pia devotione deserviit."*[20] The glory of St. Joseph, who acted as an earthly father for Jesus, is that he did this for the only-begotten Son— one hears the echo *"ex Patre natum ante omnia saecula"*—and now *"natum de Maria Virgine."* The same contrasting construction is to be heard a few days later on the solemnity of the Annunciation: *"in Unigeniti tui incarnatione. . . ."*[21]

In short, Latin can say "only Son" if it wants to, in the expression *"Filius unicus."*[22] If it says *"Unigenitus,"* it wants to say something more. Cumulative effect: In twenty-five texts a word vital for orthodox faith has virtually disappeared from the proposed translation.[23]

---

19 OP, December 21.

20 POG, St. Joseph.

21 POG, Annunciation.

22 Indeed, not only was this said in the biblical translations of the *Vetus Latina*, as was noted above in note 13, but this expression is also used in some of the earliest forms of the Roman baptismal Creed. What is significant here is that the expression was thought inadequate to express Nicea's christology. This story can be followed by consulting the index under "*monogenes*" in Kelly's *Early Christian Creeds*, op cit., 443.

23 This is a statistic gathered only from close examination of Segment Two. In the whole Missal of Paul VI the word occurs 111 times. Cf. *Concordantia verbalia Missalis Romani: Partes euchologicae* (Münster: Aschendorff, 1983), 2670-2674. For some sense of its use in the previous Missal, cf. A. Pflieger, *Liturgicae orationis concordantia verbalia, prima pars: Missale Romanum* (Freiburg im Breisgau: Herder, 1963), 697-699.

I have spoken about the importance of the translator's getting the tone right. An example of this can be found in the ending of the Easter Prefaces (*eschatol*). All of the Easter Prefaces from Easter I to Pentecost have the same ending and are rendered with the same English in the proposed translation. However, both stylistically and theologically the proposal seems to impoverish the original.

LATIN	PROPOSED TRANSLATION
Quapropter, profusis paschalibus gaudiis, totus in orbe terrarum mundus exsultat. Sed et supernae virtutes atque angelicae potestates hymnum gloriae tuae concinunt, sine fine dicentes:	Therefore, the universe resounds with Easter joy, and the choirs of angels sing the endless hymn of your glory:

What the English calls "the universe" is much more exuberant in the Latin: "*totus in orbe terrarum mundus.*" The feeling here is something to the effect of "the whole world round the globe." "Easter joy" is the English for "*profusis paschalibus gaudiis*"—again, a much less exuberant rendering. One might want to argue that these are stylistic and not theological objections, but at a certain point style is what expresses theology. There is a sheer exuberance in the Latin text that must be successfully translated, for this exuberance is expressing a *theological* insight into the celebration of the paschal mystery.

The Easter Prefaces are recited during the fifty days of the season. Should the decision to translate *"paschalibus"* as "Easter" not be considered more carefully? Would not the expression "paschal joys," repeated day after day for fifty days, be important for the instruction of all the faithful precisely at this point in the eucharistic liturgy, where the paschal sacrifice is offered? This is how words come to mean something. The word at the end of the Preface is meant to echo off of the expression at the beginning of every Easter Preface: "when Christ became our Paschal sacrifice."[24]

As part of the exuberance of these Preface endings, specific ranks of the angel choirs are mentioned: namely, *"supernae virtutes"* and *"angelicae potestates."* This comes out simply as "the choirs of angels."[25] But the translation has also missed a beautiful nuance and distinction which the Latin draws between the praise on earth and the praise from the angels. This is expressed in the relation between *"quapropter"* and *"sed." "Quapropter,"* correctly translated as "therefore,"[26] expresses very strongly that the reason for rejoicing on earth

---

24 This is to leave unmentioned that "paschal joys" is accompanied by a very strong adjective: *"profusis paschalibus gaudiis."* Thus the meaning is something like "the whole world round the globe exults with unrestrained paschal joys."

25 See note 11, above, on how frequently the specific ranks of angels are untranslated.

26 "Wherefore" would be more precise.

is because of the aforementioned things accomplished on there—i.e., some various way of expressing the paschal mystery. But what is wonderful—the exuberance continues to the very end—is that even ("*sed et*") the angels are rejoicing about what has happened on earth. So it is not merely the angels singing the praise they have always sung, but even they are rejoicing about the paschal mysteries accomplished on earth.

We can take up now yet another category of problem. In speaking of the mysterious world of the liturgy, I mentioned among its frameworks the articulation and coordination of different times. This has often been judged perhaps too subtle or complicated to translate, but I wonder. As a translator I must be willing to go over my drafts again and again, continually asking whether I can approach more closely the meaning of the original. My concern here can be illustrated in the Prayer Over the Gifts and the Prayer After Communion on the Twelfth Sunday in Ordinary Time. In the first of these we read the following:

LATIN	PROPOSED TRANSLATION
Suscipe, Domine, sacrificium placationis et laudis, et praesta, ut, huius operatione mundati, beneplacitum tibi nostrae mentis offeramus affectum. . . .	. . . that its [the sacrifice's] working may cleanse us from sin and make our hearts a gift pleasing to you.

Commenting only on verb times, we can see that in Latin there are two: having been cleansed by the sacrifice's working, *then* may we offer our hearts as a pleasing gift. In the English these are just stated one after the other, and thus the connection between them is not as tight. It is just a request for two different things. The active role of the assembly has also been lost in what is proposed. The Latin has "then may we offer," but the proposed translation has the working of the sacrifice making our hearts a pleasing gift. This is more passive than the Latin. And "offer" is a big word which carries a great deal of theological weight. It is a lot to lose in a short text like this.

In the Prayer After Communion, four times are reduced to one or two in the English:

LATIN	PROPOSED TRANSLATION
Sacri Corporis et Sanguinis pretiosi alimonia renovati, quaesumus, Domine, clementiam tuam, ut, quod gerimus devotione frequenti, certa redemptione capiamus.	Lord, we are nourished and made whole by the sacred body and blood of your Son. Grant in your kindness that the mystery we devoutly celebrate may bring us to the fullness of redemption.

The translator must recall that this prayer concludes the communion rite and looks to the dismissal of the assembly. Having been made new (one verb time) by the nourishment of the sacred body and precious blood,[27] the prayer is now (second verb time) for mercy to be certain to arrive at a future redemption (third verb time). English simply says, "Lord, we are nourished and made whole. . . ." The present tense is odd at this part of the rite.[28] In any case, there is no obvious connection between this declarative statement—stating information which presumably the Lord is not in need of—and the petition which follows it. In the second half of the prayer something is said about our habitual and devoted enacting of these rites—very condensed in "*quod gerimus devotione frequenti.*" (This is the fourth verb time.) The prayer is for mercy that we may one day seize, as a certain redemption, what we celebrate again and again in the rites. The English does not pray for mercy, nor throw into relief the contrast of habitual celebration and an eventual certain seizing of redemption. It has, more simply, "Grant in your kindness that the mystery we devoutly celebrate may bring us to the fullness of redemption." The introduction of the word "mystery" here is a good solution to the too-condensed "*quod gerimus.*" But the word "*frequenti*" is not represented in the translation, and so the precise kind of time of this present tense—the present tense of our whole lives—is not rendered.

---

27 The adjective "*pretiosi*" is not translated.

28 One could also wonder if "made whole" is strong enough for "*renovati.*"

Furthermore, to have made *"mystery"* the subject of the clause robs the assembly once again of its active role. The assembly is the active subject in the Latin. We are begging for mercy that we may do active seizing. It is not exactly a question of the Lord doing something in his kindness, but of the assembly doing something with the mercy—a stronger word than kindness—for which it is asking.

In my general description of the translating task, I spoke of letting the original language inspire my use of my own language. This will result in a certain style that English would not have on its own.[29] This deviation from the normal patterns of language as communication is common to the dynamic of what anthropologists label "sacred languages." Contact with the divine draws us out of ordinary speech. And so the translator should not hesitate to deviate from the ordinary in order to achieve religious or spiritual effects.[30] I think that in translating the Roman Missal the vernacular achieved should exhibit some sort of consanguinity with the Latin. Often I do not detect this kind of bond with Latin in the proposed

29 This does not mean, however, that the English does not have to flow with perfect ease. On the other hand, it should be remembered that, theoretically at least, English could be improved by its contact with Latin, indeed with any other language. This was certainly the case with the biblical translations of the Elizabethan age. Quite apart from what he did theologically, Cranmer's translations of the Latin prayers also brought something to English as a language.

30 For a very fine analysis of this kind of language, cf. Christine Mohrmann, "Sacred and Hieratic Languages," in *Liturgical Latin: Its Origins and Character: Three Lectures* (London: Burns and Oates, 1959), 1-26.

translation, with the result that sometimes English expressions are used that seem quite foreign to the Latin style, a style which in the end expresses an *ethos* of worship. For me, the following are examples of jarring style or of missed opportunities for developing a language particular to the world of the liturgy.

"Make our hearts dance for joy" is the way the Opening Prayer on the solemnity of the Ascension begins. This is an extremely jolting expression within the *ethos* of the Roman rite, and on such a great solemnity. This translates "*fac nos sanctis exsultare gaudiis.*" Although it is true that etymologically "*exsultare*" can carry a sense of dancing, it does not seem to be an improvement on the more traditional translation of this word. Thus, something like "make us exult with holy joys" is more fitting to the tone of this solemnity.

"Impart to us more fully" for "*perfice in cordibus nostris*" is certainly the loss of a traditional way of praying, but also theologically inaccurate for the object "*spiritum adoptionis.*" The spirit of adoption has not been partially imparted to us in such a way that it could be more fully imparted. The prayer is that it be brought to completion or perfection in us.[31]

---

31 OP, Nineteenth Sunday. Elsewhere (OP, Saturday Fourth Easter) the Latin "*perfice paschale sacramentum*" is rendered as "keep alive within us the paschal mysteries." There is considerable difference between "keep alive" and "bring to completion."

In one prayer "*caelesti lumine*" becomes "light from on high." Then "*puro intuitu*" becomes "clear minds"; and "*digno affectu*" becomes "deep affection."[32] This is a systematic elimination of sacral language easily reproduced in English: heavenly light, pure minds, worthy affection. A clear mind is not being groggy in the morning. A pure mind is something considerably different. One hears the phrase "to hold your name in . . . lasting affection" and puzzles over what Latin could stand behind this. Such puzzlement alerts the translator that something is not right in the tone. The Latin is more simple, speaking of having both "*timor*" and "*amor*" for the Lord's holy name. This is simply reverence and love.[33]

A petition in a Prayer After Communion rings with a sense of "never heard anything like that before in the liturgy": "transform us into the Christ we have received." This is meant to render "*quatenus in id quod sumimus transeamus.*"[34] The English is too didactic, too explanatory; it sounds odd and jarring. The Latin is more discreet, and such discretion would be likewise effective in English. The Latin is neuter and refers to "*perceptis sacramentis*" earlier in the prayer. The sense is that we may become what we have received.

Some expressions are soft, too sweet, even trendy for what the Latin feels like and says. "Under your caring eye" for "*sub tuae protectionis auxilio.*"[35] "Enfold us in your gracious care and

---

32 PAC, Epiphany.
33 OP, Twelfth Sunday.
34 PAC, Twenty-seventh Sunday.
35 OP, Saturday, Fourth Week of Easter.

mercy" for the much more robust and solid "*multiplica super nos misericordiam tuam.*"[36] "Foster your life within us" for "*fac nos proficere.*"[37] "Enable us to cherish" for "*fac nos amare,*" or "enlarge within us" for "*da nobis augmentum.*"[38] Or simply, "bounty" for "*abundantia pietatis tuae.*"[39] "You who give us life and purpose" substitutes for the strong divine titles "*Auctor et Gubernator.*"[40] "To reach that happy day of salvation" for "*ad tantae salutis gaudia pervenire.*"[41] "That we may celebrate with untroubled hearts" for "*ut purificatis mentibus celebremus.*"[42] "Unseen God" is odd for "*invisibilis Deus,*" and it is not precise since a thing can be visible but unseen. "Invisible" is a word which speaks of the nature of God. "Unseen" does not speak on this level.[43] "Our departed brothers and sisters" for "*famulos tuos defunctos*" not only loses the forceful image of "servants" but also calls them "ours" rather than "the Lord's."[44]

This is the cumulative effect of which I speak. I no longer recognize the inner voice of the Latin, and its content appears to be on shifting sands.

---

36 OP, Seventeenth Sunday.
37 PAC, Twenty-ninth Sunday.
38 OP, Thirtieth Sunday.
39 OP, Twenty-seventh Sunday.
40 OP, Eighteenth Sunday.
41 OP, Third Sunday of Advent.
42 POG, December 23.
43 OP, December 29.
44 POG, the Commemoration of the Faithful Departed 2; and PAC, the Commemoration of the Faithful Departed 3.

V. Summary and the Spiritual Dimensions of the Translating Task

I conclude by drawing, from what has been said, six state-ments which summarize what I have wanted to suggest. I present them for your further discussion: for dispute or, if agreed, for exploring their consequences.

- The translator must search for the inner voice of the text, which is heard in the delicate interplay between content, tone, and special vocabulary.

- The translator must be aware of the theological syntax that is operative in the "zone" surrounding a text to be translated and identify how particular dimensions of the Latin express this syntax and rely on it.

- We need a vernacular equivalent to the specialized nature of liturgical Latin: particular vocabulary and syntax, and a coherence that allows constant cross-reference and layer-ings of meaning.

- We need a liturgical vernacular that expresses a deepened and digested insight, inspired by doctrine, of what the biblical text says—in short, special language that echoes both Scripture and doctrine but is neither of these.

- We need a liturgical English that expresses and accomplishes in its own way the same tone and feeling expressed and accomplished by the Latin.

- Failure to conceive adequately any or all of these will result in a cumulative erosion of the original product to be delivered in translation.

Our discussion to this point has involved us in many grimy dimensions of the work of translation, a work that requires the combination of any number of competencies and sensitivities. May I conclude by suggesting a further dimension that needs to be considered in a discussion on the principles of translating liturgical texts: namely, its spiritual dimensions? This is not one more dimension to add alongside what has already been mentioned, but rather something that ought to permeate the whole through and through. I do not intend to develop this at length but instead to offer three images for conceiving this dimension.

The first image I would offer is the translation of the Hebrew bible into Greek—the production of the Septuagint. Of course, on one purely natural level this translation would have come about through the hard effort of individual translators who did their best to render the Hebrew in another language. But wonderful stories surround the production of this translation to indicate its inspired nature. Indeed, the seventy translators, each of which was said to produce an identical Greek text, gave their name to the product:

Septuagint.[45] This account was a way of expressing the belief of the Jewish community of the diaspora that the translation was undertaken as a sacred work and that God's desired results were achieved. It also indicates the community's fear that things could have turned out otherwise. The Jews wanted a pure translation, and that it could have been produced with this sort of agreement was a kind of miracle for them.[46] The first Christian community instinctively adopted this faith stance of the Jewish diaspora and in the Septuagint—that is, in a translated text—had its own first encounter with the Revelation of God as accomplished in Israel. This should give us hope: Revelation can be carried in translation. But it should also alert us to the fact that translation is risky business for which divine assistance is required. Furthermore, translation has a communal dimension, represented first in the seventy, whose agreement on the text was an assurance for the rest of the community that counted on finding the Word of God in it.

Coming to the Latin tradition, the figure of St. Jerome comes immediately to mind. He offers not so much an image of translating's communal dimensions as much as a vision of

---

45 The original number of seventy-two came to be rounded down to seventy in most accounts.

46 Clearly I am speaking here not about what we know concerning the actual production of the text, but rather of the meaning of the "myth" that surrounds its production. For a fine study of the actual translation and the stories surrounding it, cf. Mogens Müller, *The First Bible of the Church: A Plea for the Septuagint* (Sheffield, United Kingdom: Sheffield Academic Press, 1996). This study is full of implications for how we should conceive the task of biblical translation.

what is required of an individual translator. His irascible personality may likewise offer us hope in our present struggles. His figure gives a kind of permission to care passionately about the questions involved. But it was not his irascibility as such that produced the Vulgate. It was its energy turned inward on himself, where he learned to demand of himself all the hard work, the asceticism, required for accomplishing what he rightly assessed as a most holy undertaking. Jerome had gradually become convinced of the so-called Hebrew verity, actually rejecting the Septuagint. He became convinced of the need to produce a Latin translation that would exactly reproduce the Hebrew of the Old Testament. He was confident that such translation could be done, and he went to immense pains to ensure the accuracy of his text. Even though his rejection of the reliability of the Septuagint is questionable for both theological and ecumenical reasons, we still have in him the image of a translator spurred on by a sense of the urgency of his undertaking. Thus did he produce a version of the Scriptures which for centuries mediated Latin Christianity's encounter with the revealed Word. And it was precisely by letting his own Latin be influenced by the Hebrew that he "raised the vulgar Latinity of Christians to the heights of great literature."[47]

---

47   J. N. D. Kelly, *Jerome: His Life, Writings, and Controversies* (New York: Harper & Row, 1975), 163. For discussion of Jerome as translator, cf. 141-167.

Someone might be inclined to object that these are stories surrounding the translation of the Scriptures, not of liturgical texts. But this is to miss a point to which we are perhaps too little sensitive: namely, that the liturgy is a primary carrier of Revelation for the Christian community. It is in the liturgy that the Scriptures achieve their livingness and the fullest context for their interpretation. This interpretation *is* the Tradition, which also makes sense not as free-floating abstract ideas but only as founded in the same liturgy.[48]

When we think that in translating Latin liturgical texts we are translating a language that has carried Revelation for a large and extensive Christian community for more than a thousand years, we ought thereby to be made aware that we are dealing with something very sacred. We must pray for inspiration and agreement among the "seventy" translators, an agreement that cannot be achieved without divine help.

I would offer a final image that unites these communal and individual dimensions of the translating task. I am thinking of the iconographer. You are probably aware of the habit of

---

48 This does not mean that the liturgical assembly is above the Tradition or the Scriptures. Rather, it is there to receive both as what comes to us from the apostles, represented in the bishop's presence at the head of the assembly, either in person or in one whom he has ordained. *Dei Verbum*'s careful articulation of these various realities needs to be understood as especially manifest in the liturgy: "Thus it is clear that, by God's wise design, tradition, scripture and the Church's magisterium are so connected and associated that one does not stand without the others, but all together, and each in its own way, subject to the action of the only Holy Spirit, contribute effectively to the salvation of souls" (no. 10; my translation).

speech in which an iconographer is said "to write an icon," not to paint it. This is intended to express that the icon is meant to be a visual expression of the Sacred Scriptures, a visual version of Tradition, as it were. Thus, the goal of the artist is not the achievement of some new and original expression. It is, rather, to be a living expression for a living community of what Scripture and Tradition have already said. Hence, the iconographer—or let us call him a trans-lator—is subjected to strict canons in color, design, subject matter. These may at first seem to be narrowing in their effect, but in fact they ensure that it is Scripture and Tradition that he is translating and not simply a personal, and therefore idiosyncratic, vision. Iconographers genuinely devoted to the customs of their high art know that they must fast and pray while they are working; and generally they ask the community for whom they are writing the icon to fast and pray as well. In this way they put their hard-won skill at the disposition of the Spirit so that from their translation the Spirit's message may flow. Thus a surprising and wonderful livingness emerges from the icon, the translated piece. In the great icons something highly original emerges, but it emerges precisely in the effort not to be original but to be faithful to the canons.

Let us pray that holiness and talent and competence may continue to come together, and come together ever more fully in the Church in the United States, so that we may produce a magnificent icon: a liturgical vernacular, wholly inspired and indeed something new, and yet familiar like the icons which have been written before us. Faith that comes to us from the apostles!

PASTORAL ISSUES IN THE TRANSLATION OF LITURGICAL TEXTS

STANISLAUS CAMPBELL, FSC

Introduction

Twenty years ago this month the editors of the periodical *Worship* devoted the entire November issue to the topic of language in the liturgy. In the introductory article of that issue, entitled "Language in the Liturgy: Where Angels Fear to Tread," associate editor Don Saliers touched on a number of the issues then confronting—and I would submit still confronting—both Catholic and Protestant churches in the provision of adequate liturgical texts. He concluded the article by saying,

> We must continue in the midst of an ongoing prayer to search for language befitting both its transcendent and anthropological aims. It must delight and move and, above all, have a capacity to form and to express the deepest affections and virtues belonging to the word and mystery of God's self-communication.[1]

---

1   Don E. Saliers, "Language in the Liturgy: Where Angels Fear to Tread," *Worship* 52 (1978): 488.

I am neither a Latinist nor one engaged in the provision of texts for the liturgy; but as one who participates in liturgy daily, either liturgy of the hours or Eucharist or both, and as one who is somewhat conversant with the history and nature of the Church's worship, I will address some issues in the English translation of Latin liturgical texts as these pertain to the needs of participants in the liturgical act—both the needs they have for personal expression of their faith in the words of the liturgy, and for their personal formation by means of those same words in an ever-deepening participation in the mystery of Christ. In other words, I will attempt to speak in part to pastoral issues of language in the liturgy—language which, in the words of Don Saliers just quoted, has "a capacity to form and to express the deepest affections and virtues belonging to the word and mystery of God's self-communication." These issues of language, these pastoral issues, I suggest, must be considered along with those others pertaining more directly to the establishment of hermeneutics for the translation of Latin liturgical texts into English based on the assumptions "that a sacred language system with vernacularizations was the goal of the Council" and "that Latin as a sacred language will be maintained in such fashion as to remain the base language for communication within the Church."[2]

---

2   Dennis D. McManus, "Principles of Translation: Issues in the Application of the Hermeneutics of *Comme le prévoit*," *BCL Newsletter* 30 (June/July 1994): 25.

I see six issues here, which I will simply name as principles before treating each one in some detail:

1. Translated texts draw all those engaged in liturgy to as full as possible an active participation in it.
2. Translated texts respect the narrative form of liturgical prayer.
3. Translated texts are appropriately metaphoric.
4. Translated texts incorporate inclusive language.
5. Translated texts are substantial enough for repeated use as prayer over a lengthy period of time.
6. Translated texts respect the principle of organic growth.

So let us turn now to an examination of each of these issues.

I. Translated Texts Draw All Those Engaged in Liturgy to as Full as Possible an Active Participation in It

This issue, stated here as a principle, may seem at first hearing not to be an issue at all. Who would dispute it? In fact, however, when we consider other issues surrounding *translation* of liturgical texts, this principle may at times yield to other concerns. Should it?

The overarching principle enunciated by the *Constitution on the Liturgy* is stated in its article 14:

In the restoration and development of the sacred liturgy the full and active participation by all the people is the *paramount concern*, for it is the primary, indeed the indispensable source from which the faithful are to derive the true Christian spirit.[3]

This English version of the text translates the Latin "*summopere*" as "paramount concern." Other English versions render it as "the aim to be considered before all else."[4] Thus, the *Constitution* makes "active participation" that which everything else in the reform and the renewal of the liturgy must promote. What has often enough not been well considered is the nature of "active participation." Article 30 of the *Constitution* makes clear that active participation is more than the utterance of words, the performance of gestures, and the assumption of postures:

> To develop active participation, the people should be encouraged to take part by means of acclamations, responses, psalms, antiphons, hymns as well as by actions, gestures and bodily attitudes.[5]

---

3   Second Vatican Council, *Sacrosanctum Concilium* (*Constitution on the Sacred Liturgy*), no. 14, in Austin Flannery, ed., *Vatican Council II: The Conciliar and Post Conciliar Documents*, vol. 1, new rev. ed. (Northpoint, N.Y.: Costello Publishing, 1996). Emphasis added. Henceforth cited as SC.

4   *Constitution on the Sacred Liturgy: Second Vatican Council, Dec. 4, 1963* (Collegeville, Minn.: Liturgical Press, 1963); "Vatican Council II: Constitution on the Liturgy," in *Documents on the Liturgy 1963-1979: Conciliar, Papal, and Curial Texts* (Collegeville, Minn.: Liturgical Press, 1982).

5   SC, no. 30. Emphasis added.

Thus, the audible words and sensible gestures are *means* to what the *Constitution* suggests is a further level of engagement. "That further level of engagement," according to the late Professor Mark Searle,

> is engagement in the invisible realities signified by the visible rite, namely, the exercise of the priestly office of Jesus Christ before the throne of God in the power of the holy Spirit.

> To participate, then, is to allow oneself to become caught up in the eternal relationship of the Son to the Father, a relationship which was enacted in the incarnate life and death of the Son of God and is summarized in the term "paschal mystery." It is a relationship into which we are introduced when we were first engrafted on to the living body of the Church in baptism, which we live out day by day in persevering obedience to the Spirit, and which we rehearse as a people in the weekly celebration of the Eucharist on the Lord's Day.[6]

Article 48 of the *Constitution* makes it abundantly clear that the words and actions of the liturgy (and here, specifically, those in the Eucharist) are but means to engagement in the mystery signified by these words and actions. It says,

---

6   Mark Searle, "The Mass in the Parish," *The Furrow* 37 (1986): 622.

The church, therefore, spares no effort in trying to ensure that, when present at this mystery of faith, Christian believers should not be there as strangers or silent spectators. On the contrary, having a good grasp of it [i.e., the mystery of faith] *through* the rites and prayers, they should take part in the sacred action, actively, fully aware, and devoutly.[7]

It would seem, then, that all liturgical texts uttered or heard by people participating in liturgy should have the capacity to draw them into the mystery which the words in some way signify. True, the *Constitution* is not speaking explicitly here of the presidential prayers. But how can the acclamation "Amen," of which it *is* speaking here, uttered as consent to the prayer proclaimed by the priest or the one presiding mean anything at all if one has not been interiorly engaged in the meaning of the words uttered or heard?

I doubt that there is disputing among us that the texts of the liturgy should draw us into the mystery it is celebrating. The dispute, if it comes, will be over characteristics of specific texts or over the adoption of certain principles, such as

---

7   SC, no. 48. Emphases added. The Latin text reads: "*Itaque Ecclesia sollicitas curas eo intendit ne christifideles huic fidei mysterio tamquam extranei vel muti spectatores intersint, sed per ritus et preces id bene intellegentes, sacram actionem conscie, pie et actuose participent.* . . ." Most other English versions of the *Constitution on the Sacred Liturgy* available in the United States mistranslate the section of article 48 quoted here. For a consideration of the problem see my "Liturgical Catechesis and *Sacrosanctum Concilium,* Article 48," *Proceedings of the North American Academy of Liturgy—1995* (Valparaiso, Ind.: NAAL, 1995), 101-104.

"dynamic equivalence," which are perceived, according to one's point of view, either to help or to hinder this deeper participation. For example, in 1978 Fr. Aelred Tegels, then the managing editor of *Worship*, commented, "It seems to me that the prayer over the gifts for the feast of All Saints approaches nadir."[8] The English text reads as follows:

> Lord,
> receive our gifts in honor of the holy men and women
> who live with you in glory.
> May we always be aware
> of their concern to help and save us.
> We ask this. . . .[9]

The Latin reads:

> *Grata tibi sint, Domine, munera,*
> *quae pro cunctorum offerimus honore Sanctorum,*
> *et concede,*
> *ut, quos iam credimus de sua immortalitate securos,*
> *sentiamus de nostra salute sollicitos.*
> *Per Christum. . . .*

---

8   Aelred Tegels, "Chronicle," *Worship* 52 (1978): 77.

9   ICEL, *The Sacramentary* (New York: Catholic Book Publishing, 1975).

Fr. Tegels remarked,

> As those who read Latin will note, the ICEL
> [International Commission on English in the Liturgy]
> translation seriously distorts the meaning of the orig-
> inal. The Latin text speaks of the saints as being
> "concerned for our salvation," while the ICEL text
> presents them, in effect, as saviors.[10]

The text, by its misrepresentation of the role of the saints,
could hinder engagement in the mystery by someone paying
close attention to it because it distracts such a worshiper from
involvement in the prayer and causes that person to wonder
how Jesus Christ's unique salvific role can somehow be that
of the saints. In the case of Fr. Tegels, it would seem that the
text did hinder his own active participation in the liturgy at
the point of proclaiming it, for he commented that texts like
this are "distressingly inadequate in general and sometimes so
poor that it is embarrassing to be required, as chief celebrant,
to read them publicly."[11] Fortunately from one point of view, I
suspect most people don't give close enough attention to the
text to notice the misrepresentation. On the other hand,
infelicitous statements like this, even going unnoticed, may
still have an effect on people without their realizing it, especially if these statements are numerous and encountered
regularly. If serious enough, over time, these inadequacies

---

10   Ibid.
11   Ibid.

could hinder, more or less, a full engagement in the mystery because they depict aspects of it falsely or inadequately.

A number of critics of our current translations have commented on what they see as just such a pervasive inadequacy in the texts. It is what they call the "pelagianizing" of the texts, or the Pelagian or semi-Pelagian tendency of the texts. One critic has written,

> Very many of the ICEL translations ask God to "help" us do something, the implication being that basically we can do it ourselves but would like his assistance to ensure success. . . . [T]he theologically precise and objective language of the Roman collects never asks God to "help" us do something; the words are always *fac, tribue, concede, da, praesta,* and the like.[12]

Let us take as an example the Opening Prayer for the Sixth Sunday in Ordinary Time. The English reads:

God our Father,
you have promised to remain for ever
with those who do what is just and right.
Help us to live in your presence.
We ask this. . . .[13]

---

12 Richard Toporoski, "The Language of Worship," *Communio* 4 (1977): 247. This article appeared also in a somewhat abbreviated form in *Worship* 52 (1978): 482-508.

13 *The Sacramentary* (1975), op cit.

The Latin text reads:

> *Deus,*
> *qui te in rectis et sinceris manere pectoribus asseris,*
> *da nobis tua gratia tales exsistere,*
> *in quibus habitare digneris.*
> *Per Dominum. . . .*

Other critics of this tendency recognize, fairly, that this "pela-gianizing" is not intended "but is rather the result of single-minded concern for simplicity and clarity."[14] Nevertheless, the repeated rendering of prayers in this fashion can create a cast of mind which reinforces a tendency all too prevalent in North American society that achievement of almost every-thing comes through personal effort, assisted sometimes by the efforts of others. We are hindered, then, from entering through the liturgical text into the mystery of salvation which is accomplished not by our efforts with some divine help but by the grace of God in the paschal mystery of the life, death, and resurrection of Jesus Christ and our graced union with him in that same mystery.

It is important to note here that while these criticisms are directed to current translations, the texts approved for the newly proposed translation of the Sacramentary seem remark-ably less prone to hinder active participation understood primarily as engagement in the mystery of Christ. Let us look

---

14   Aelred Tegels, "Chronicle," *Worship* 58 (1984): 444.

at the counterparts of the two texts just examined, the Prayer Over the Gifts for the Feast of All Saints and the Opening Prayer for the Sixth Sunday in Ordinary Time:

> Be pleased, Lord, with the gifts we offer
> in honor of all the saints.
> We believe they have reached the haven of eternal
> life;
> grant that we may experience their prayers for our
> salvation.
> We ask this. . . .

> O God,
> you promise to remain with those
> whose hearts are faithful and just.
> By the gift of your grace
> make our lives worthy of your abiding presence.
> We ask this. . . .[15]

Let's turn now to the second issue, which is intimately related to the first one we have just considered, in that it provides a way for liturgical prayer to enable active participation as I have described it.

---

15 ICEL, *The Sacramentary* (Washington, D.C.: ICEL, 1997). This text has not yet been affirmed by the Holy See. Further passages quoted from the Sacramentary are drawn from this translation, unless otherwise noted.

II. Translated Texts Respect the Narrative Form of Liturgical Prayer

Like many texts of the Scriptures, many prayer texts of the liturgy have a narrative form. By narrative form I mean a linguistic structure in which a story is told or elements of a story are related. This form is especially evident in many Prefaces of the Eucharistic Prayer, in Eucharistic Prayer IV, and, in an attenuated manner, in many Collects or Opening Prayers of the Mass wherein the story of God's wondrous deeds, the *mirabilia Dei*, in the history of salvation are recounted or alluded to. From the point of view of participants in the liturgy, this form is especially conducive to encountering the transcendent God, to strengthening the bond of union between them and their Lord, and to uniting them among themselves in Christ because the story is told "in the language of 'you' and 'we.'"[16] In other words, by the use of first- and second-person pronouns in the narration, those of us who hear the story realize our involvement in it. God's story and our story merge. Recall, for example, the Preface of Eucharistic Prayer II in the words of our current translation:

> *Father*, it is *our* duty and *our* salvation,
> always and everywhere
> to give *you* thanks
> through *your* beloved Son, Jesus Christ.

---

16 Helen Kathleen Hughes, *The Language of the Liturgy: Some Theoretical and Practical Implications* (Washington, D.C.: International Commission on English in the Liturgy [ICEL], n.d.), 6.

He is the Word through whom *you* made
    the universe,
the Savior *you* sent to redeem *us*.
By the power of the Holy Spirit
he took flesh and was born of the Virgin Mary.

For *our* sake he opened his arms on the cross;
he put an end to death
and revealed the resurrection.
In this he fulfilled *your* will
and won for *you* a holy people.[17]

Or consider the proposed translation of the Opening Prayer for the Mass of the Twenty-third Sunday in Ordinary Time, wherein the attenuated narrative appears in the subordinate clause:

God of unfailing mercy,
who redeemed us and adopted us as your children,
look upon us with tender love,
that we who believe in Christ
may enjoy true freedom
and enter our promised inheritance.
We ask this. . . .[18]

---

17 Emphases added.
18 Emphasis added.

Biblical narrative, and I believe we can say the narrative form of liturgical prayer so akin to it, has the power to be instrumental in revealing the transcendent God and to facilitate an encounter with this God whereby a divine claim is established on the praying community.[19] Likewise, narrative in Bible and liturgy tells the story of the praying community; and, as Sr. Kathleen Hughes has observed, when that kind of narrative constitutes the prayer of the community, the community

> describes itself, its needs, its aspirations, its understanding of its role in the work of building the kingdom. Moreover, through its prayer the community enters into a relational universe: it discovers its fundamental structure as gathered Church, naming and acknowledging God in response to God's initiative, presenting itself before God in union with its mediator, Jesus Christ.[20]

The narrative character of liturgical prayer evident in the Latin texts of the Roman liturgy has been preserved, for the most part, in the English translations of these texts, but some have asked how well preserved. If the narrative character of liturgical prayer is so important for the encounter with God in the mystery which is at the heart of this prayer, could the current English translations more adequately present this

---

19 For a discussion of this function of biblical narrative, cf. William C. Placher, *The Domestication of Transcendence: How Modern Thinking About God Went Wrong* (Louisville, Ky.: Westminster John Knox Press, 1996), 186-189.

20 Hughes, op cit., 13.

character than they do? The question is particularly acute with respect to the translations of those classic Roman collects which, in the interest of a direct style, avoid the mention of or allusion to God's deeds in a subordinate clause—thus, in the eyes of ICEL's critics, avoiding a direct and clear relationship of the *mirabilia Dei* to the petition as the grounds upon which that petition is made. I recognize that ICEL struggled mightily in its early years with the challenge of translating the collects. I am aware that the spare use of words and succession of simple sentences which typify most of the 1973 versions pleased many, but I am also aware that some of the harshest criticism ICEL has received centers on its manner of translating the collects.[21] It seems to me that the controversy will continue since many of the texts for the new edition of the Sacramentary, while fuller and more literal, still may not employ subordination sufficiently. And yet it must be recognized that ICEL seems to have been responsive to its critics in establishing as one of its principles of revision with respect to structure and style "an openness to use a more complex English syntax" presupposing "respect for the needs of proclamation." And, indeed, besides the version quoted above, one can find other instances of relative clauses grounding the petitions of Opening Prayers.[22]

---

21 Cf. Toporoski, op cit., 251-253; Tegels, "Chronicle" (1984), op cit., 443.

22 ICEL, *An Interim Report on the ICEL Revision of the Sacramentary, 1982-1994* (Washington, D.C.: ICEL, n.d.), 14. For Opening Prayers utilizing subordinate clauses see, for example, those for the Second and Fourteenth Sundays in Ordinary Time in the 1997 version of the Sacramentary.

Whether recognized or not by participants in liturgy, preservation of—even enhancement of—the narrative form of liturgical prayer would seem important, if not essential, to that active participation understood as engagement in the mystery; and thus syntactical forms, such as the subordinate clause, which may enhance the narrative form of certain euchological texts might be given further consideration and debate.

We turn now to the third issue, which I present also as a principle.

III. Translated Texts Are Appropriately Metaphoric

A liturgiologist recently observed that "to experience Christian liturgy is to enter a jungle of metaphors."[23] Metaphor in the liturgy is not confined to verbal statements. The non-verbal elements and the whole of a liturgical service can be understood as metaphoric.[24] For our purposes here we will focus on metaphor in the translated, verbal proclamations of the liturgy.

While a liturgical celebration is certainly the praise, thanksgiving, self-offering, and petition of the Church in Christ to God, the Father, it is also what has been termed a "commu-

---

23 John Witvliet, "Metaphor in Liturgical Studies: Lessons from Philosophical and Theological Theories of Language," *Liturgy Digest* 4:1 (1997): 7.

24 Cf. Mark Searle, "Liturgy as Metaphor," *Worship* 55 (1981): 98-120.

nications event."[25] In our culture, where the scientific mode of knowledge and what John Shea has called "flatminded literalism" prevail, the communications process of the liturgy can be misunderstood as a "process of conveying information." Understanding the nature of metaphor and entering into the liturgy as a whole and its various elements as metaphorical can enable us, in the memorable words of Romano Guardini, to "relearn a forgotten way of doing things and recapture lost attitudes"[26] and so engage in the liturgical act, which is that active participation in the liturgy understood as engagement in the mystery which it embodies. The less precise, tensive language of metaphor, which is more open, ambivalent, and rich in associations than the denotative language of everyday prose, allows this to happen.

We need not take the time here to dwell on how metaphor allows this to happen. There have been numerous studies in recent years on metaphor and symbol and the processes by which they function in worship.[27] What is important to note, I think, is that in the translation of Latin liturgical texts where metaphoric language occurs in the original, it should be preserved in some way in the translation—but also, where untraditional and overly precise language is used in the Latin, a translator would be doing a service to render it more metaphorically in English. Let me illustrate the latter.

---

25 Ibid., 98.
26 Romano Guardini to Msgr. J. Wagner, letter, 1 April 1964, reprinted in *Assembly* 12 (1986): 322-324.
27 Cf., for example, the bibliography in *Liturgy Digest* 4:1 (1997): 108-122.

The Latin text of the *anamnesis* section of Eucharistic Prayer IV reads in part: "*offerimus tibi ejus Corpus et Sanguinem, sacrificium tibi acceptabile et toti mundo salutare.*" One could translate that rather literally, as ICEL has done for the current translation of the Sacramentary, as "We offer you his body and blood, the sacrifice which brings salvation to the whole world." ICEL has chosen for the new translation of the Sacramentary—rightly, I think—to soften the overly precise statement of what is offered by rendering the sentence as "We offer you the sacrifice of his body and blood, an offering acceptable to you, which brings salvation to all the world." Such a rendition is, to use the words of ICEL in a note regarding this text, a "more 'sacramental' mode of expression" and certainly a more traditional way in which to speak of what is being offered. For what is being offered is not only the Body and Blood of Christ, but ourselves in, through, and with him to the Father.[28] The evocative, metaphoric language of the Roman Canon, Eucharistic Prayer I, is witness to this traditional way of referring to the offering: "*Panem sanctum vitae aeternae et Calicem salutis perpetuae,*" which in the ICEL version has at least minimally enough of its metaphoric character preserved as "the bread of life and the cup of eternal salvation." Such language invites those participating to see themselves caught up in the one sacrificial offering of Christ, because the holy bread and the salvific cup, explicitly mentioned here, are symbolic of their very own lives, too.

---

28   ICEL, *Third Progress Report on the Revision of the Roman Missal* (Washington, D.C.: ICEL, 1992), 93.

Augustine's famous words on this matter may be recalled here:

> For what you see is simply bread and a cup—this is the information your eyes report. But your faith demands far subtler insight—the bread is Christ's body, the cup is Christ's blood. Faith can grasp the fundamentals quickly, succinctly, yet it hungers for a fuller account of the matter. As the prophet says, "Unless you believe, you will not understand" (Isaiah 7:9). . . . So now, if you want to understand the body of Christ, listen to the Apostle Paul speaking to the faithful: You are the body of Christ, member for member (1 Corinthians 12:27). If *you*, therefore, are Christ's body and members, it is your own mystery that is placed on the Lord's table! It is your own mystery that you are receiving! You are saying Amen to what you are—your response is a personal signature, affirming your faith. When you hear "The body of Christ"—you reply "Amen." *Be* a member of Christ's body, then, so that your Amen may ring true![29]

It appears that it is often issues of orthodoxy that create the pressure to use literal rather than metaphoric language. For example, the erosion of belief in the real presence of Christ under the species of bread and wine is unsettling, to say the least, and can lead some to advocate use of language in the

---

29 From a homily of St. Augustine of Hippo (*Patrologia Latina* 38:1246-1248), translated by Nathan Mitchell in "Your Own Mystery," *Assembly* 23 (1997): 14.

liturgy which removes all ambiguity or multivalence in referring to the offering in order to counter this unbelief. But can rendering the essentially metaphoric, sacramental language of liturgy more literal to counter heresy or supposed heresy assist in achieving one of the chief purposes of liturgy? Is not the purpose of liturgy as a "communications event" to symbolically actualize the paschal mystery of Christ in ways which draw Christians into it so that they both express their commitment in faith to living this mystery and are formed in its dynamics? I submit that there are other, more appropriate, extra-liturgical ways in which to educate people regarding the orthodox teaching of the Church. Mark Searle once observed in his discussion of liturgy as metaphor,

> We are starting from the supposition that the role of liturgical language is not simply to convey supernatural "facts," but to engage us in relationship; and that the actions of the liturgy are not undertaken for the purpose of getting a job done, so much as to constitute and express attitudes. The problem would be that most people "read" the liturgy in terms of something educational and purposeful, whereas the task of the liturgist is to help them enter into it in such a way that they discover it as an encounter with mystery, generating both insight and commitment.[30]

---

30   Searle, op cit., 102.

Closely related to the issue of metaphoric language in liturgy is the question of inclusive language. That brings us to our fourth pastoral issue, here stated as a principle.

IV. Translated Texts Incorporate Inclusive Language

Inclusive language in the liturgy has been an issue for the bishops of this country since the late 1970s. I do not wish to review that history here nor to dwell on all the issues raised in those years around the stated need for inclusive liturgical language both "horizontal" and "vertical." Like metaphor, I believe, inclusive language is necessary in the liturgy. The lack of it hinders, if it does not exclude, many—both women and men—from participating actively at that deep level of engagement in the mystery which, as I stated at the start, is, according to the *Constitution on the Liturgy*, the "paramount concern" in the renewal of the liturgy.

Through the last couple of decades, ICEL has made clear its commitment to inclusive language in the translation of Latin texts and composition of new texts. The special commission on inclusive language held at the Vatican in May of 1985 and involving representatives of the Bishops' Committee on the Liturgy, ICEL, the Congregation for Divine Worship, and the Congregation for the Doctrine of the Faith seems to have established that "inclusive language referring to the liturgical assembly did not present any significant difficulties."[31] In the report of this meeting in the *BCL Newsletter* the implication was that there *were* significant difficulties with so-called "vertical" inclusive language, language referring to God.

Because, as I understand the situation, these difficulties remain, I would like to offer two reflections on the issue of "vertical" inclusive language—neither of them new—which recall some of the issues here and perhaps assist in clarifying them. Before I offer these, however, it is necessary to say that issues surrounding the translation of biblical texts for the liturgy would seem to differ somewhat from those pertaining to euchological texts. The *Criteria for the Evaluation of Inclusive Language Translations of Scriptural Texts Proposed for Liturgical Use*, adopted by the National Conference of Catholic Bishops in November 1990, contain the two major criteria, which are

> the principle of fidelity to the Word of God and the principle of respect for the nature of the liturgical assembly. Individual questions, then, must be judged in the light of the textual, grammatical, literary, artistic, and dogmatic requirements of the particular scriptural passage and in light of the needs of the liturgical assembly. In cases of conflict or ambiguity, the principle of fidelity to the word of God retains its primacy.[32]

---

31 *BCL Newsletter* 21 (1985): 19.

32 No. 7. Cf. *BCL Newsletter* 26 (1990): 38.

Translations of euchological texts may not have quite the same constriction as do translations of biblical texts to remain strictly faithful to the original languages, since they do not enjoy the guarantee of being the inspired word of God. Translators of liturgical prayers, I submit, would have the primary, but not exclusive responsibility to respond to the pastoral principle enunciated in the *Constitution on the Liturgy*. I say "not exclusive" responsibility because a translator of a liturgical text does have the responsibility to convey the meaning of the text she or he is translating, but always with an eye to enabling active participation. That said, let us turn our attention to the two reflections on "vertical" inclusive language.

First, it is a truism to say that many women and not a few men find it difficult and annoying to participate in a liturgy in which masculine imagery only is used of God. In the area of the country in which I live, I am witness to what seems to be a fairly widespread grassroots movement which has changed the wording of the response before the Prayer Over the Gifts from the current official form, using masculine pronouns for God, to one which says

> May the Lord accept the sacrifice at your hands
> for the praise and glory of *God's* name,
> for our good, and the good of all *the* [or *God's*] Church.

The same grassroots movement has substituted "God" for "him" in the words of a portion of the Preface Dialogue: "It is right to give him thanks and praise." These unauthorized moves, which create some discordance in a congregation not of one mind on the matter, do not seem to be the result of some bold feminist initiatives, but the response of ordinary people to suggestions of those already more sensitive to exclusive language or to appealing practice seen elsewhere. The introduction of these attempts at gender-neutral language for God seems to have occurred very much in the manner by which the now widespread practice of holding hands at the "Our Father" has become popular. Neither this manner nor that of a presider substituting the word "God" for every occurrence of the word "Father" in the official text are conducive to promoting for all people that active participation in the liturgy as I have been describing it.

Does not, however, the locally widespread phenomenon of substitution for and elimination of masculine imagery for God in liturgical texts suggest that some of the language employed in these texts may be, at least, inadequate? And lest this phenomenon be thought the only grounds for more inclusive vertical language, ought we not to recognize that there are maternal images of God in the Scriptures, and that saints such as Bernard of Clairvaux, Brigid of Sweden, and Anselm of Canterbury, among others, all speak of the motherhood of God?[33]

---

33 Cf., for example, Anselm of Canterbury's prayer to Jesus as mother: "But you, too, good Jesus, are you not also a mother? Are you not a mother who like a hen gathers her chicks beneath her wings? . . ." Quoted in Elizabeth Johnson, *She Who Is* (New York: Crossroad, 1996), 150. Cf. also Luke 13:33-34.

It is true that when we speak of translations of Latin texts, it may seem that not much can be done to render the English more inclusive if the English is to be faithful to the Latin of which the terms used for God are more exclusive. A greater inclusivity in language may seem to be confined to the composition of *original* texts. But there are instances when even in translation, more inclusive terms in English can be used for less inclusive terms in Latin when speaking of God and our relationship to God. ICEL, for example, has done this in reversing an earlier decision to render "Deus" as "Father" in presidential prayers. The new versions will use "non-gendered language for God in so far as possible, and the translation of *Deus* as 'God'. . . ."[34] This practice occurs frequently in the new translations for the Opening Prayers of the Mass.[35] While the gender-neutral term "God" has the advantage of avoiding the masculine term "Father," and of being a more literal translation of "*Deus*," it has the double disadvantage of using an inherently non-personal term to address the personal God and of removing metaphoric language from the

---

34 ICEL, *Interim Report*, op cit., 20 (C, 8). This is not the only example of ICEL's effort for a more inclusive language relating to God. The introduction to the *Third Progress Report on the Roman Missal* states: "Over the course of the 1980s, ICEL also studied the question of masculine language used of God. In the revisions an effort has been made to keep the title 'Father' in most instances wherever the Latin has *Pater* but to remove what many have criticized as the gratuitous introduction of the title 'Father' into many of the translated prayers found in *The Roman Missal* of 1973. Where doctrinal or linguistic considerations allowed, the revisions have avoided the use of masculine pronouns to refer to the First and Third Persons of the Trinity. In both the translated and original prayers an effort has been made to use a larger variety of titles and images for God in order to open up a greater sense of the mystery and majesty of the Godhead" (10).

35 Cf., for example, the Opening Prayers for the Second, Fifth, Sixth, Seventh, and Ninth Sundays in Ordinary Time.

prayers which, as already noted, ought to characterize them. In fact, this use of the word "God" might be considered, from the point of view which values the metaphoric character of liturgical prayer, a noteworthy deficiency in the new translations—a deficiency which is not present in the current texts using the word "Father" modified by such adjectives as "almighty," "everlasting," "all-loving," and the like. Mark Searle has observed that

> to speak of old age as autumn is clearly a metaphorical usage, but when God is spoken of as "he" or as "Father" or as "Savior" the metaphorical character of such discourse is easily overlooked.[36]

For this reason, Ian Ramsey stresses the role of what he calls "qualifiers." Words such as "infinite," "everlasting," "immortal" and "all-loving" are not words which have any recognizable human experiential referent. In fact, their role is rather to deny any such reference to the words such as "Father," "Lord," or "Savior" which they qualify. Thus to speak of God as an all-loving Father or an all-powerful Savior is to deny any real continuity between God and any human experience of the role of father or savior. In this way, through simultaneous assertion and denial, through juxtaposition of claim and disclaimer, the transcendence of the reality of which we speak is safeguarded.

---

36 Searle, op cit., 118.

From a pastoral point of view, however, some trade-offs are probably necessary in the matter of inclusive versus exclusive language. So many women and not a few men are put off from that active participation, that deep engagement in the prayer of the liturgy, by the predominantly masculine imagery or metaphors for God in our liturgical texts that it seems essential to strive for some kind of balance if for no other reason than the pastoral one of promoting that deeply engaging active participation. That brings us to my second reflection on the issue of inclusive language.

Besides allowing for greater and more fruitful participation in the liturgy on the part of many, better utilization of "vertical" inclusive language, where it can occur, in translations of liturgical prayers and certainly in original compositions would allow for more diverse, less limiting images of God. Is it necessary that all masculine imagery in Latin liturgical prayers be transposed to their vernacular versions? Would it not be possible to maintain at least dynamic equivalence between Latin and English texts either in omitting some of this imagery or in replacing it with feminine or gender-neutral imagery so long as what is signified by the images is, if not formally equivalent to the Latin, complementary and surely not contradictory? How else will a balance among sets of images in *translated* texts be achieved? And is not an achievement of such a balance a desirable goal from the point of view of the overarching pastoral principle that active participation is of "paramount concern" in the renewal of the liturgy?[37]

ICEL has striven to provide in the new translations for the Sacramentary a greater variety of images and titles for God. Not all of these have found their way into the final versions. Let us look at a couple of samples. The Latin text for the Opening Prayer of the Second Sunday of Lent reads:

Deus, qui nobis dilectum Filium tuum audire preacepisti,
verbo tuo interius nos pascere digneris,
ut, spiritali purificato intuitu,
gloriae tuae laetemur aspectu.
Per Dominum. . . .

In 1992 ICEL proposed rendering this text as follows:

Gracious God,
you instructed us to listen to your beloved Son.
Nourish us inwardly with your word of life
and purify the eyes of our spirit,

---

37 See the remarks of Dennis McManus in his keynote address to the NCCB at the study day on liturgical translations, June 23, 1994: "There is no absolute answer to the question of 'literal' versus 'liberal' translation styles. If the goal of the vernacularization is to faithfully present a tradition of Christian life, then each passage must be judged individually for its ability to be rendered best. On some occasions, a literal translation will prove most powerful and faithful in presenting the sense of the Latin original; on other occasions, a literal translation will obscure or even destroy the message offered in the sacred language. The development of hermeneutics which carefully guide the vernacularization process generally is a task of the highest importance." In *BCL Newsletter* 30 (June/July 1994): 25.

that we may rejoice in the sight of your glory.
We ask this. . . .

It seems to me there was an attempt here to modify the stark, perhaps kingly imagery, suggested by "*Deus . . . praecepisti*" in the English rendition "Gracious God, you instructed. . . ." The final version, however, reads more literally:

O God,
who commanded us to listen to your beloved Son,
nourish us inwardly with your word of life
and purify the eyes of our spirit,
that we may rejoice in the sight of your glory.
We ask this. . . .

The Latin text of the Opening Prayer for the Twenty-third Sunday in Ordinary Time is

Deus,
per quem nobis et redemptio venit et praestatur adoptio
filios dilectionis tuae benignus intende,
ut in Christo credentibus
et vera tribuatur libertas et hereditas aeterna
Per Dominum. . . .

It seems to me that the new English version proposed for the Sacramentary, which we looked at earlier, has seized on the imagery of a loving parent present already in the Latin text and emphasized it:

God of unfailing mercy,
who redeemed us and adopted us as your children,
look upon us with tender love,
that we who believe in Christ
may enjoy true freedom
and enter our promised inheritance.
We ask this. . . .

That achieving a balance in imagery might be important, consider these remarks which appeared a few years ago in a description of inclusive language:

Serious questions must . . . be raised about the "normative" character of male imagery for God, even though such images appear routinely in the Bible. To raise such questions does not represent infidelity to either scripture or tradition. Rather, it is simply a recognition that historical texts reflect cultural *contexts*, which in turn represent the androcentric interests and patriarchal prejudices of human authors. (The Bible, after all, is God's Word in human words, as Vatican II's decree on divine revelation, *Dei Verbum*, carefully pointed out [no. 120].) Ironically, the exclusive use of male metaphors for God (King, Lord, Master, Prince, Father)—however understandable historically—may today produce the (surely unintended) result of *limiting* the revelation of God's being and action. Such a limitation would be profoundly contrary to both scripture and tradition, which argue that Divine being and action are *limitless*, that God wishes *all* to be saved and to come to a knowledge of the truth.[38]

I would take the author of that text, when speaking of "*limiting* the revelation of God's being and action," to mean that the limiting occurs from a human perspective and that there is no limit on God's own self-communication.

We can conclude these observations with the words of Janet Walton:

> Concerns about inclusive language provide a serious critique of sacramental practice. They challenge the post-conciliar church to examine the theology and ecclesiology embodied in the celebration of sacramental liturgies so that the significance of these moments reflects more honestly the fullness of divine/human relationships.[39]

Having gone, on that issue, where angels should fear to tread, let me move on to the next issue, again stated as a principle.

---

38 Nathan Mitchell and Martin Connell, "Inclusive Language," *Liturgy Digest* 1:2 (1994): 100.

39 Janet Walton, "Inclusive Language," *The New Dictionary of Sacramental Worship*, ed. Peter E. Fink (Collegeville, Minn.: Liturgical Press, 1990), 598.

V. Translated Texts Are Substantial Enough for Repeated Use as Prayer over a Lengthy Period of Time

It seems to me that our euchological texts must be rich enough to yield new insights, new attitudes with repeated use. Familiarity with the texts ought not to be onerous, but be that which enables ever greater access to the inexhaustible mystery celebrated in the liturgy. If the texts are too "thin" and yield up all their meaning in one reading, this access will be difficult if not denied altogether. Perhaps a personal experience will illustrate what I mean.

Recently, in preparing for the liturgy of the Twenty-first Sunday in Ordinary Time, I looked at the Opening Prayer for the Mass and read

> Father,
> help us to seek the values
> that will bring us lasting joy in this changing world.
> In our desire for what you promise
> make us one in mind and heart.
> Grant this. . . .

The content seemed "thin," the petition abrupt and without grounds, and the tone semi-Pelagian by virtue of the verb "help." The word "values" also triggered my curiosity. What Latin word or phrase could that be rendering? So I turned to the Latin original and found

Deus,
qui fidelium mentes unius efficis voluntatis,
da populis tuis id amare quod praecipis,
id desiderare quod promittis
ut, inter mundanas varietates,
ibi nostra fixa sint corda,
ubi vera sunt gaudia.
Per Dominum. . . .

I was surprised at how much more there was to ponder here than in the English version, how the petition for unity in English was actually the statement in Latin that grounded the petition—and, as expected, that there was not a hint of a semi-Pelagian attitude. I thought surely a rendering of this text which captured more of the Latin phraseology and syntax would be more engaging than the one we currently have. It was a pleasant surprise to discover that the new translation of this prayer reads

O God,
you inspire the hearts of the faithful
with a single longing.
Grant that your people
may love what you command
and desire what you promise,
so that, amid the uncertain things of this world,
our hearts may be fixed where true joys are found.
We ask this. . . .

Perusing other collects in their current English versions, Latin originals, and new English versions, I discovered a pattern similar to the one seen here: from creating an English version employing a direct style and exhibiting dynamic equivalence with the Latin original, ICEL has moved, in the new versions, to a more complex style and to more formal equivalence with the Latin. While the 1973 versions were undertaken with pastoral motives in mind, I cannot help thinking that the new versions, as ones rendering the content of the Latin texts more fully, will be able to better nourish those who pray them.[40]

Many years ago Richard Toporoski, among others, observed that among what John S. Kenyon has called the "functional varieties" of English, the language of worship traditionally falls in a variety used for formal platform or pulpit speech and public reading, not in the variety comprising colloquial language used for "familiar conversation, private correspondence, formal conversation, [and] familiar public address."[41]

---

40 Both critics and friends of ICEL need to bear in mind what ICEL correctly acknowledges: "As is well known, the present prayers of the *Missale Romanum* are taken from a variety of sources and represent different stages in the history of liturgical prayers. A number of the prayers, particularly for Sundays and the major solemnities, are ancient. Others are, for example, from the Middle Ages, from seventeenth and eighteenth centuries, and from the period following the Second Vatican Council. The question of the content of the prayers is extremely important, but the variety of their sources and the different historical periods they represent raise at least some question about the theological consistency of the body of texts as a whole. Some of the prayers make profound theological statements; others do so to a lesser degree. Care must be taken not to invest certain prayers with a theological depth or exactness that may have been imposed on them by a later age." *Consultation on Revision: The Roman Missal: Presidential Prayers* (Washington, D.C.: ICEL, 1982), 9-10.

41 Toporoski, op cit., 229.

ICEL, he feared, had for whatever reason mistakenly used the colloquial variety instead of the formal variety and in so doing had broken with a universal tradition. For human beings, he said,

> be they Catholics or Protestants, Christians or non-Christians, have never worshiped in the contemporary conversational or colloquial idiom of their own vernacular. Sometimes, as we know, they have not worshiped in their own vernacular at all, but when they have, there has always been a stylized functional variety of their vernacular which they have used.[42]

ICEL, in his opinion, might have been attempting to be faithful to that passage in the 1969 *Instruction on the Translation of Liturgical Texts* (*Comme le prévoit*), which reads,

> The language chosen should be that in "common" usage, that is, suited to the greater number of the faithful who speak it in everyday use, even "children and persons of small education."[43]

Some phrases in this excerpt are from an allocution of Pope Paul VI, and Toporoski notes that in that allocution the pope

---

42 Ibid., 231.

43 Consilium for the Implementation of the Liturgy, *Instruction: Translation of Liturgical Texts* (*Comme le prévoit*), no. 15, in *Documents on the Liturgy, 1963-1979: Conciliar, Papal, and Curial Texts* (Collegeville, Minn.: Liturgical Press, 1982), nos. 838-880. Henceforth to be cited using internal paragraph numbers.

made it clear that by language in common usage he did not mean the language of the streets. Pope Paul said,

> It is always necessary nevertheless, as you well know, that it [the vernacular] be worthy of the very lofty matters which are signified by it and different from the daily manner of speaking which flourishes in the streets and markets, such that it may touch the emotions and inflame hearts with the love of God.[44]

I do not know if ICEL has listened to its critics on this matter, but the new translations for the Sacramentary have been rendered in the more formal style advocated by Toporoski and others. The question now from the pastoral point of view is this: Are these fuller translations better able to engage ordinary people in the liturgy, leading them to a deeper participation in it? Probably only time will tell; but objectively speaking, the richer texts would seem to invite closer attention and more reflection, unlike the 1973 versions composed in a much more direct style, which sometimes either yielded meaning too quickly or were not even heard because of their brevity and directness or because of poor proclamation.

---

44 Paul VI, "Allocutio Summi Pontificis ad Participantes 'Conventum de Popularibus Interpretationibus Textuum Liturgicorum,'" *Notitiae* 1 (1965): 379. English translation from Toporoski, op cit., 257.

Having rich, full texts serves a characteristic important in ritual prayer forms, and that characteristic is familiarity. If the liturgy, generally, and liturgical texts, specifically, are meant, among other purposes, to nourish, form, shape, and direct the lives and the personal prayer of those who engage in liturgy, the euchology of the liturgy needs to be substantial so that it may bear repetition without losing effectiveness—or better, bear repetition which enables greater insight, deeper expression of faith, and more profound formation in affections and virtues of life in Christ. The need for familiarity demands that some texts, more than others, remain unchanged or little changed over a fairly long period of time. The Eucharistic Prayers and most parts of the Order of the Mass, the psalms, the optional psalm prayers, and the orations in the four-week psalter of the Liturgy of the Hours would be included here. Most people over time memorize many of the common texts of the liturgy, which enables them to enter into the entire liturgy less preoccupied with the texts themselves and more focused on their meaning. Many also internalize the words of frequently used texts, including those of Eucharistic Prayers, so that what these texts convey shapes the very fabric of their lives. It would be a disservice to the flow of liturgy and to the spirituality which it can and does inculcate for translators to alter familiar texts too easily or too frequently.

I believe Kevin Irwin has captured something of the importance of familiar rites and texts in his *Context and Text: Method in Liturgical Theology*. Speaking of the pre-conciliar liturgy he writes,

Ritual familiarity enabled people to participate in liturgy in such a way that the non-variability of the rite led to the distinct, very desirable prospect that the communion with God experienced through the liturgy was *supported* by familiar rites, not *dominated* by them. The kind of prayer experienced rested on but also transcended rubric, symbol, or text. Liturgy was not self-conscious since the rites were pr[e]scribed. Diligent care was to be expended in executing them. By contrast, the present liturgy can lead to ritual self-consciousness because the legitimate variety now invited by the present reform can allow "liturgical performance" (admittedly a poor phrase)—how gestures are executed, how symbols are used, and what words are used in prayers—to become almost too important.

The legacy of the former Roman rite invited a level of liturgical participation that transcended the particular rites and words in order to draw participants into an experience of the divine that is almost a contemplative stance before and in God. In this case language becomes merely a prop that discloses and unleashes meanings both verbally and nonverbally.[45]

---

45 Kevin W. Irwin, *Context and Text: Method in Liturgical Theology* (Collegeville, Minn.: Liturgical Press, 1994): 202.

That is not to say, however, that the words and rites of the reformed liturgy cannot do the same. The Advisory Committee of ICEL was certainly aware of the importance of familiarity with certain texts of the liturgy when, in 1989, it adopted guidelines for revision of texts in the Order of Mass which called for restraint in changing the text of ritual responses, "short prayers memorized by the people," or short texts proclaimed by presiders and inviting a congregational response. These texts were to be retranslated only for serious reasons in ways that "do not create undue pastoral problems for the assembly."[46]

One other aspect of this issue of providing rich texts for repeated use is the responsibility translators have to shape texts for *proclamation* in the liturgical assembly. Liturgical texts are not primarily destined for study or private reading. Thus, besides the needed attention to vocabulary and syntax, there must be attention "to rhythm, cadence, balance, and rhetorical effect" because the meaning and richness of the *proclaimed* text is carried by more than its vocabulary and syntax.[47] Linguists and philosophers have stated the importance of *setting* or context-in-life for the conveyance of meaning in the use of language, even insisting that setting is more decisive than vocabulary for determining meaning.[48] Those non-verbal elements of rhythm, balance, and the like

---

46   ICEL, *Third Progress Report*, op cit., 15.
47   Ibid., 7.
48   Cf. A. C. Thiselton, *Language, Liturgy and Meaning* (Bramcote: Grove Books, 1975), 3-4.

as part of the setting in which liturgical texts are proclaimed are *important*, then, for the transmission of their meaning. It is for this reason, it seems, that ICEL insists on proclaiming aloud in committee all draft translations as they are being developed.[49]

We come now to the final pastoral issue, again stated as a principle.

VI. Translated Texts Respect the Principle of Organic Growth

Article 23 of the *Constitution on the Liturgy* states an important directive which pertains directly to translated texts:

> Finally, there must be no innovations unless the good of the church genuinely and certainly requires them, and care must be taken that any new forms adopted should in some way grow organically from forms already existing.[50]

Translated liturgical texts are new forms constituting what one might call the first steps in organic growth of the linguistic dimension of liturgical rites. To put it in terms used by

---

49 Cf. ICEL, *Interim Report*, op cit., no. 8, p. 12 and p. 16 (part two, n. 7). For studies on the non-verbal elements of translated liturgical texts, cf. John B. Foley, "An Aural Basis for Oral Liturgical Prayer," *Worship* 56 (1982): 132-152; Michael Hodgetts, "Sense and Sound in Liturgical Translation," *Worship* 57 (1983): 496-513.

50 SC, no. 23.

the Congregation for Divine Worship and the Discipline of the Sacraments, "the first significant measure of inculturation is the translation of liturgical books into the language of the people."[51] If these texts are not as faithful as possible to their originals, then it would seem that organic growth is jeopardized. "To be as faithful as possible to their originals" does not mean to be slavishly literal. The *Instruction on the Translation of Liturgical Texts* of January 25, 1969, had this often quoted statement regarding vernacular translations from Latin:

> The translator must always keep in mind that the "unit of meaning" is not the individual word but the whole passage. The translator must therefore be careful that the translation is not so analytical that it exaggerates the importance of particular phrases while it obscures or weakens the meaning of the whole.[52]

It is precisely around this issue of organic growth that controversy exists. Some would insist on more "literal" translations while others promote "dynamic equivalence." Both groups seem to have a concern for this organic growth as well as a pastoral concern. The first group, which might be termed the "literalists," seems to wish that as much of the detail in the Latin originals, including the form of the texts, be preserved lest any of the meaning be lost and the faithful deprived of

---

51 *Inculturation and the Roman Liturgy* (usually cited as *Varietates Legitimae*), 1994 (Washington, D.C.: United States Catholic Conference, 1994), no. 53.

52 *Instruction* (*Comme le prévoit*), op cit., no. 12.

their rightful inheritance. Proponents of this view have maintained that content exists only in form, and so to change the form is to change the content.[53]

The promoters of "dynamic equivalent" texts, on the other hand, taking the 1969 *Instruction* seriously, seem to acknowledge that contemporary ecclesial and cultural conditions demand that Latin texts be rendered more simply and directly in the vernacular, without thereby becoming discontinuous with the Latin originals, if they are to transmit the substance of the original meaning to people today. ICEL, as we know, has promoted this view, appealing to the 1969 *Instruction on Translation* and, with respect to prayers, to the

> belief that a vernacular liturgy risked being too word-oriented with the result that congregations would be overwhelmed with words, that the texts would be taken for granted, and that proper attention would not be given to the thoughts the prayers were meant to convey.[54]

But is it possible that both of these views might really embrace this organic growth? And why is this organic growth important for the expression and formation of the faith of those who participate in liturgy? Let's look at each question. Recognizing that the 1969 *Instruction* is currently held in

---

53 Cf. Toporoski, op cit., 235.
54 ICEL, *Consultation on Revision*, op cit., 6-7.

disfavor by some, I submit that it is possible for both views—that of the literalists and that of the promoters of "dynamic equivalence"—to embrace organic growth. Translation utilizing formal platform speech and not that for more familiar public address may appear to be more easily a development respecting organic growth. Translation in this mode is more literal, with greater use of syntactical constructions identical or similar to those of the original texts. But translation which is "dynamically equivalent" to the original may, at times, be preferable to a more literal or formal rendering because it sets forth the central meaning of the original texts in a way which allows hearers better, more direct access to it. The more formal may sometimes obfuscate, thus impeding organic growth; the more liberal may sometimes clarify, thus furthering this same growth. Decision as to which mode of translation to use could be made on a case-by-case basis.

As to the second question—why is this organic growth important for the expression and formation of the faith of those who participate in liturgy?—it seems one could respond in the following vein: Organic growth is pastorally important because liturgy as ritual gives symbolic expression to what is at the heart of the communal life of the Church, becoming the principal vehicle for the transmission of the Church's tradition. Too great a discontinuity or disruption in its forms from one age to another carries the great risk of distorting what the liturgy should signify and thus causing it to cease to be both a fit expression of the faith of the Church and an appropriate means for deepening that faith in the lives of those who participate in the liturgy.

The ancient (fifth-century) axiom of Prosper of Aquitaine (c. A.D. 440), "*legem credendi lex statuat supplicandi*," and its subsequent use in the history of the Church are a witness to the pastoral need for this organic growth. The axiom initially indicates that the rule of prayer should establish the norm for belief. Its meaning, more freely rendered as "*lex orandi, lex credendi*," has often been expanded to express the notion that liturgy is formative of the life of faith for believers, and this would be in keeping, it seems, with the meaning of the original adage. This longstanding teaching supporting the notion that liturgy is formative, and not only expressive of the life of faith, would seem to be reason enough for the organic development of text and rite in the Church's worship.

Conclusion

In conclusion, let it be said that the six principles identified here as pastoral issues in the translation of liturgical texts are issues which, it seems to me, must be considered if new hermeneutics for translation are to be developed based on the twin assumptions "that a sacred language system with vernacularizations was the goal of the Council" and "that Latin as a sacred language will be maintained in such fashion as to remain the base language for communication within the Church."[55]

---

55   McManus, op cit., 25.

Article 14 of the *Constitution* stated quite emphatically that the "paramount concern" or "aim to be considered before all else" in the restoration and promotion of the liturgy is the "full and active participation by all the people." All the issues examined here have been viewed in the light of this overarching principle. And we have seen that by "active participation" the Council meant more than external participation. In fact, it meant primarily that *internal* participation in the paschal mystery which is at the heart and center of every liturgical action. I submit that whatever the new hermeneutics may be which are developed for the translation of liturgical texts, they must serve this overarching pastoral principle and the principles directly related to it. We must, in the words of Don Saliers quoted at the beginning,

> continue in the midst of an ongoing prayer to search for language befitting both its transcendent and anthropological aims. It must delight and move and, above all, have a capacity to form and to express the deepest affections and virtues belonging to the word and mystery of God's self-communication.[56]

It is certainly my hope that competing views on issues of translation may be reconciled so that we may all move forward together in preserving what needs to remain and in developing what needs to grow for the sake of our common worship in spirit and in truth—a worship that is not on the periphery but at the very core of our life together in Christ.

---

56   Saliers, op cit., 488.

SUMMARY, SYNTHESIS, AND DIVERGENCE

DENNIS D. MCMANUS

Introduction

It is no easy task to summarize—let alone synthesize—the excellent points raised by the three principal presenters at the Forum. In addition, the many public discussions of the bishop members and guest observers among themselves were also of very high quality. The following account, therefore, aims only to make a brief summary of the main points of each presenter, followed by a general synthesis of all three of their viewpoints as they were discussed in the final two sessions of the Forum.

Summary of Presenters' Points

Each of the guest scholars represented important positions on the nature of liturgical language generally, and on liturgical translation in particular. Their respective theses were extremely engaging and given with clarity and conviction. The following is the briefest of summaries of those theses, set out here only for the later purpose of drawing them together in an experimental and partial synthesis.

Fr. Gil Ostdiek, OFM, opens his address by asking how we might do better at "the shaping of prayer texts in the vernacular." He approaches this question, as he puts it, "from the point of view of the assembly"—i.e., the worshiping community in the parish, which must listen to and pray the vernacular texts of the Mass. Ostdiek divides his topic into four subdivisions: prayer texts, contexts, inculturation, and liturgical translation. Each of his principal points is reviewed here.

Liturgical Texts as Prayer Texts—In speaking of liturgical texts as *prayer* texts, Ostdiek first draws attention to the fact that all liturgical texts are, more than anything else, prayer texts of a given assembly using them in the present moment to offer their praise and thanksgiving, as well as their petitions to God. For such texts to be successful, Ostdiek argues, they must provide images (biblical ones, in particular) that connect with modern life in a way that is both beautiful and memorable for the sake of lasting influence. In an extended reflection, Ostdiek helpfully notes that liturgical texts are only just now being examined by those branches of the social sciences that "explore in detail the sensory and physiological basis of how our inner human pro-cesses of knowing and communication occur." Surely such an avenue of investigation can only improve the future translation and composition of texts for the liturgy.

Second, he writes that the prayer text is "to be the prayer of the assembly," which uses it while "gathered [in the] here and now." In short, there is no liturgical text which is somehow ideal apart from its being prayed by the local church, allowing its words "to become the genuine prayer of the congregation" in which "each of its members should be able to find or express himself or herself." Such prayers have an awesome duty: "to speak to [the] assembled people, draw them into prayer in God's presence, and evoke their faith and their Christian commitment to live as disciples sent into today's world." Ostdiek cautions that more attention must be given to the *narrative* quality of our prayers, i.e., to how they tell "the story of God's saving deeds in their own lives." Only then, it would seem, can a true connection be made between liturgical prayer and the liturgical assembly.

Third, Ostdiek remarks that "the liturgy's prayers are proclaimed and heard; they are by their very nature oral/aural." This is a key element in his thinking, repeated frequently in his paper. Liturgical texts have been subject, he writes, to "too much attention . . . questions about fidelity and precision, and too little attention to [their] suitability for oral proclamation and hearing." This is an especially important component of liturgical prayer in its duty "to feed the sacramental imagination of the faithful." Ostdiek urges that the notion of orality—as a way of understanding the profound impact that the spoken word has upon the life of the listener—be explored continually for its application to the work of translation. He concludes this section eloquently by asking, "Would this not be a worthwhile area to explore in a future agenda dealing with liturgical translations that bring the riches of the English cultural heritage to the implanting of God's reign in our midst?"

Contexts—Borrowing from the language of anthropology, Ostdiek next proposes that liturgical language or prayer texts can only be understood within their "complex symbol system," which has "multiple historical-cultural contexts." For Ostdiek, the primary context for a liturgical prayer is the liturgical ritual action it accompanies.

Second, he states that this idea of word-and-ritual "can be expanded by noting that the words of the liturgy are deeply woven into an interlocking web of other symbolic forms of communication—inflection and tone of voice, facial expression, gesture, posture, movement, space, and environment." He writes in sum: "The agenda for furthering the work of liturgical translation would be well served by an exploration of both the ritual context and the complex system of signs which form the larger field of discourse in which the translated texts are embedded."

Third, Ostdiek states that "discerning the meaning to be brought forward in translating a Latin text requires locating it in its original context." But the retrieval of such meaning—a meaning that often varies in its own historico-literary context—naturally raises the question for the translator: "Which *stage* of meaning is to be taken as the authentic one?" Texts, writes Ostdiek, may be "multivalent" with meaning. In such a case, how does one find a way forward? How is the translator to choose a single meaning for a given passage when confronted with such complex contexts? Ostdiek concludes that the solution is found by enlarging "our working understanding of the liturgy as constituting a vast repertoire of prayer texts which collectively, rather than individually, proclaims the fullness of the faith to us."

Inculturation—Here, Ostdiek asserts that vernacular translation is clearly an example of inculturation as originally understood by the Second Vatican Council, since living languages lie at the heart of living cultures: "the living language of a people (*sermo vivus*) is a preeminent means (*praecipuum instrumentum*) of communication among them." Next, Ostdiek turns his attention to asking, "What . . . is inculturation and how does it happen?" He answers insightfully by reminding the reader that, in fact, inculturation is a two-way process: "Inculturation is a double movement, involving a gradual, dialogical process in which a culture is christianized [sic] and Christianity is incarnated in a culture, assimilating compatible values of the culture." Third, Ostdiek extends his reflection on the dynamics of inculturation to include "the collaboration of all who have a role in the process of inculturation." He reminds us, in the words of John Paul II, that inculturation is a slow journey. Ostdiek concludes by suggesting that the *General Directory for Catechesis* provides a model for a theological understanding of inculturation and the pastoral process it requires.

Translation—Unlike other forms of translation, liturgical or prayer translation is unique, according to Ostdiek, who quotes the instruction *Varietates Legitimae* to state that such translation "has its own special characteristics: It is deeply impregnated by the Bible; certain words current in Latin use (*memoria, sacramentum*) took on a new meaning in the Christian faith. . . ." He goes on to remark that a dual task faces the translator who would offer vernacular language to the Church: translators must develop "a companion cate-chesis which breaks open the meaning of these words in our prayer, but without interrupting that prayer or distracting people from it."

Second, Ostdiek urges that liturgical translation is not a matter of rendering one word for another but—in the language of linguistic anthropology—of rendering a "system of relationships" where, building on an understanding of the deep structure of language, "the semantic relationships of the two languages can meet." He concludes, in a major observa-tion, that as a result of these insights from linguistic anthro-pology, both of these related sciences now understand that "authentic translation must work in great measure on the principle of dynamic equivalence."

Third, Ostdiek reminds the reader of the original intention of the Second Vatican Council and the Consilium for the Implementation of the Liturgy during the first years of the reform of the liturgy, in which it was thought best that episcopal "conferences sharing a common language share a common text." He observes that, as a result, any agenda addressing the issues of liturgical translation must be dealt with in an international manner. As was previously done in Rome 1965 with Paul VI's invocation of the international translators' conference, Ostdiek questions whether the present moment would not also benefit from a second, similar gathering to begin to address problems in English translation of the liturgy, "joined by [scholars] from all the major modern languages."

On a concluding note, Ostdiek pleads with those who would make every translation issue into a moral one. He cites Robert Weschler's acclaimed study, *Performing Without a Stage* (North Haven, Conn.: Catbird Press, 1998), as a resource for approaching the ethical dimensions of liturgical translation. Ostdiek implicitly warns against the tendency to pass moral judgments on translators whose approaches might disagree from our own. It is an issue, he insists, for both the literary and the ecclesial worlds.

Fr. Jeremy Driscoll, OSB, offers his perspectives from two important background experiences. First, a significant portion of his own scholarly and academic work has somehow involved the Fathers of the Church, particularly in his translation of many patristic works into English. Second, for several years, Driscoll has served as an advisor to the Bishops' Committee on the Liturgy, reviewing various fascicles of the Roman Missal translation submitted to the U.S. bishops' conference by the International Commission on English in the Liturgy (ICEL). He shapes his overall approach to his paper around this question: "What perspectives do I have on the task of translating the Missal given this background[?]"

Driscoll arranges his thoughts in five categories: (1) the task of a translator of patristic texts, (2) the application of the lessons of a patristic translator to the translation of the Roman Missal, (3) identification of the broad issues facing the translator of the Roman Missal, (4) consequent reservations about the 1997 ICEL translation of the Roman Missal, and (5) the spiritual dimensions of the translator's task.

Translating Patristic Texts—Driscoll begins his discussion of translation by arguing the foremost principle he has discovered in rendering patristic texts: that a translator must "be conscious of and extremely sensitive to" the larger context in which the work was written. He develops three components, in particular, in this method: (1) an appreciation for "the way in which whatever is ex-pressed has been rendered in the particular genius of that language"; (2) an accurate retrieval of the "tone or feeling" of the whole piece, without which a "whole world of thought and feeling which are inextricably intertwined" would be lost to the reader; and (3) a careful attention paid to vocabulary, or those particular "words which carry the burden" of the text in a distinctive way. As a part of his method as a translator, Driscoll states, "I will not be afraid to let the original language suggest new possibilities in mine, pushing it to places it may not go on its own initiative." He refers to the entire process as "searching for the inner text or the inner voice of the text." He concludes this section helpfully by underlining that such a translation method helps the reader to detect the *specific differences* in the texts that open up the possibility of their relevance to modern Christian life.

How This Could Apply to Translating the Roman Missal—
The Roman Missal's texts are intended for liturgical use: they are oral and proclaimed, not written and read. As a result, Driscoll notes that "one is translating a text to be used in contemporary worship, and to some extent history and difference create a gap that needs to be bridged." It is in the service of bridging that very same gap that he then suggests that first and foremost, the translator of the Roman Missal must "understand the text exactly in its own language." As well, this means "appreciating the particular genius with which that language has expressed something. It likewise includes detecting the tone or feeling of the whole." Lastly, the same attention paid to the importance of vocabulary in the translation of patristic texts must be brought to bear on the Roman Missal as well.

What Are the Translation Issues in the Roman Missal?—
Driscoll centers his thoughts here on the concept of "mystery," which he defines as "concrete 'somethings' within which a divine reality is concealed." Through contact with such mysteries, the divine life that they mediate is participated in by the believer. Liturgical language counts among these very mysteries, for doesn't it also make for communion

with God? In effect, Driscoll states, everything that is liturgical is "referential, referring to something" that ultimately relates to the final mystery: union with the life of the Trinity itself. The translator, to be fully in tune with this world, must then "try to name and identify as many of" the syntactical components that the expression of mystery generates in the language of the Roman Missal. By "syntax" Driscoll refers not merely to the order of language alone, but more broadly to the world of ideas and expression of faith that unify the Roman expression of worship, as a way of holding together the unity of the Roman rite. All of this taken together creates what he then refers to as "a specific theological vision larger than a personal synthesis is likely to be."

What then does the translator need to develop in order to render this special syntax, this language of "mystery" whereby, in the Roman style, the mysteries of redemption are celebrated? Driscoll states poetically that at base what is needed "is a vernacular equivalent of this particular vocabulary, a vernacular equivalent of the syntax, a vernacular equivalent of the coherence that allows constant reference and cross-reference, permitting the mysteries to echo off of each other."

Such a system may be developed by identifying first how patristic language is constructed. To a large extent, patristic language is derived from "a particular way of reading Scripture," i.e., from the vocabulary and syntax that the Fathers constructed to create a speech that was at once biblical and summative of the ancient Rule of Faith. The language of the liturgy is developed from these two sources—the Bible and the Rule of Faith—and is thereby quite properly patristic. The liturgy that uses this language is itself the occasion at which the mysteries proclaimed in the Scriptures are realized in the assembly's worship. In turn, "the foundation for the content of faith lies in the mysterious realities achieved in the believing assembly wherein that faith is professed and celebrated." In sum, the language of the Roman Missal is a "*lex orandi* upon which a *lex credendi* is formulated." Despite the complexity of its development, the full translation of such liturgical language must constitute the translator's principal task.

Driscoll concludes this section by restating the importance of recreating the unique tone of the Roman Missal's Latin in the tone of an English vernacular. Indeed, he stresses that quite unlike the expectations of other schools of translation theory, a modern vernacular would do well to allow itself to be pushed in "new directions" by the ritual language it renders— all in service of capturing the same tone in the translation that can be found in the original.

Examples of Problems in the Proposed Translation—In this section, Driscoll outlines several specific problems that he has found in the 1997 ICEL translation of the Roman Missal. For each problem, he includes a technical discussion and, occasionally, a consideration of alternative methods of approach to the issue at hand. He declines, in principle, to offer re-translations or alternative texts per se, since this activity belongs, he writes, in "a later step in the process" of translation. Instead, he concentrates in this section on "understanding exactly" what the text means to convey in the genius of its own language, the tone proper to the piece as originally composed, and lastly, the special message of the special vocabulary in the text.

Because the limited scope of this summary does not allow for a lengthy discussion of Driscoll's highly technical points on textual problems, it must suffice to say that he concentrates on three examples whereby he can demonstrate the method of textual investigation he has just outlined.

First, he remarks at length on the importance of understanding context exactly by comparing two Prefaces, one from the feast of the Transfiguration and another from the second Sunday of Lent, which deals also with the Transfiguration event. Driscoll then reviews in detail the importance of capturing the author's intention in both texts by providing a close reading of each text for its native genius, tone, and vocabulary. In remarks critical of the 1997 ICEL rendering of these same texts, Driscoll reminds the reader of two important principles to which any translator must be alert in working with the Roman Missal: (1) that a given word may "come to mean something in the liturgy that it may not mean elsewhere"; and (2) that the effects of mistranslation—or, in Driscoll's method, of "not understanding exactly" the inner voice of the text—are *cumulative*, both on the reader and in the way in which the translator begins to see all of the texts in the Missal considered as a whole.

In a second example, Driscoll reviews the meanings of the term *"Unigenitus"* within early biblical, conciliar, and finally, liturgical settings. His discussion attempts to demonstrate how in-depth historical understanding of such *termini technici* can not be substituted in the translator's preparation of the text, and how the gradual emergence of the meaning of such terms is another example of the kind of "Roman Missal syntax" he described earlier. The failure to read the Missal texts carefully risks two grave errors, in Driscoll's analysis: first, missing the fact that a word can acquire a meaning from its repeated use within a *seasonal context* as well as a biblical or doctrinal one; and (2) key terms in the doctrinal develop-ment of the Christian faith can be unintentionally eliminated from the Missal vernacular if the translator is unaware of their subtle but differing uses in liturgical texts.

In a third example, Driscoll develops an important rule for the translator who considers the relationship between rhetor-ical form and content, or, put more simply, between style and theology. Describing the importance of translating exuberant passages in Latin with a comparable English, he writes on the problems in the phrase *"profusis paschalibus gaudiis"*: "'Easter joy' is the [ICEL] English for '*profusis paschalibus gaudiis*,' again a much less exuberant rendering. One might want to argue that these are stylistic and not theological objections, but at a certain point style is what expresses theology. There is a sheer exuberance in the Latin text that must be success-fully translated, for this exuberance is expressing a *theological insight* into the celebration of the paschal mystery."

Driscoll then turns his attention to the question of the liturgy's notion of time. It is important, he notes, to take account of verb tenses and the ways in which they sequence, in effect, the experience of the Church and the believer as petitioners for and receivers of redemptive grace. That experiential order—an order of subjective experience rather than of history—is key in first understanding and then translating what is often a tangle of verb tenses within a single prayer. Driscoll concludes his technical discussion with a corresponding insight, first mentioned in his introduction, of how important it is for him, or any translator, to allow the original language to "inspire my use of my own language. This will result in a certain style that English would not have on its own." He refers to this process as one of "bonding" between the original and the receptor languages. He concludes, "This deviation from the normal patterns of language as communication is common to the dynamic of what anthropologists label 'sacred languages.' Contact with the divine draws us out of ordinary speech. And so the translator should not hesitate to deviate from the ordinary in order to achieve religious or spiritual effects."

Summary and the Spiritual Dimension of the Translating Task— In a helpful summary section, Driscoll gives six points that encapsulate his address:

1. The search for the inner voice of the text—found in the interplay of content, tone and vocabulary—is at the heart of the translator's work.

2. Awareness of the theological syntax of a text is vital for bringing any final expression to it in a vernacular tongue.
3. A vernacular equivalent is needed for the specialized nature of liturgical Latin.
4. That vernacular equivalent "echoes both Scripture and doctrine but is neither of these."
5 A liturgical English that captures the same tone and feeling of the Latin original is an important goal of vernacularization.
6. The original text can be eroded—in its meaning, tone, style, and content—cumulatively by translators' failure to understand fully their responsibilities towards the text.

In his concluding remarks, Driscoll offers the reader a variety of reflections on the spiritual dimensions of the translator's task. He writes on how Revelation itself can be borne in translation, citing the meaning and use of the Septuagint as well as the teaching of St. Jerome as supportive examples. Perhaps Driscoll's most compelling image, however, is that of comparing the translator to an iconographer. He writes that an icon is meant "to be a living expression for a living community of what Scripture and Tradition have already said." This same goal, according to Driscoll, would be the aim of the translator: to provide the living Church with an oral and aural expression of the "Tradition" and of the Scriptures themselves. There is room here, in the spoken icon, for originality; but, as Driscoll notes, such originality "emerges precisely in the effort not to be original but to be faithful" to the canons of translation and of the liturgy itself.

Br. Stanislaus Campbell, FSC, begins his address by drawing the attention of the Forum to the fact that the issues in the translation of liturgical texts have remained, in some ways, as perplexing today as they were twenty years ago. Referring to an article by Don Saliers in *Worship*, Campbell notes that Saliers "touched on a number of the issues then confronting—and I would submit still confronting—both Catholic and Protestant churches in the provision of adequate liturgical texts." Campbell is taken with Saliers' call for liturgical language that, as Saliers states it, has a "capacity to form and to express the deepest affections and virtues belonging to the word and mystery of God's self-communication." Campbell then suggests that achieving the goal that Saliers proposed necessarily entails a look at some six issues in liturgical language, along with others, that must be addressed by translators if the vernacularization of a sacred language was the goal of the Council and if Latin was intended as the base language for communication within the Church. He then lists the issues in the order in which his paper will explore them: (1) that translated texts "draw all those engaged in liturgy to as full as possible an active participation in it"; (2) that they "respect the narrative form of liturgical prayer"; (3) that translated texts "are appropriately metaphoric"; (4) that they "incorporate inclusive language"; (5) that such texts "are substantial enough for repeated use as prayer over a lengthy period of time"; and (6) that they "respect the principle of organic growth."

Translated Texts Draw All Those Engaged in Liturgy into as Full as Possible an Active Participation—Campbell straight-away places article 14 of Vatican II's *Sacrosanctum Concilium* (*Constitution on the Sacred Liturgy*) before his reader to establish an important principle: that the goal of any aspect of the reform of the liturgy was to promote "the full, conscious and active participation by all the people." But exactly how, Campbell asks, is the much debated phrase "full, conscious and active participation" to be understood?

This is a key point if the success of liturgical translation is to be judged, based in large measure on whether it promotes this very kind of Council-inspired participation. He cites a parallel passage from *Sacrosanctum Concilium*, no. 30, that seems to fill out the qualities of this participation: "To develop active participation, the people should be encouraged to take part by means of acclamations, responses, psalms, antiphons, hymns as well as by actions, gestures and bodily attitudes."

However, to allay any criticism that such descriptions amount to formulae for mere *external* involvement with the liturgy, Campbell completes his discussion of this critical point with a reminder cited from the works of the late Mark Searle, who wrote that to participate in the liturgy "is to allow oneself to become caught up in the eternal relationship of the Son to the Father, a relationship which was enacted in the incarnate life and death of the Son of God and is summarized in the term 'paschal mystery.'" Campbell then offers a clear conclusion: any translation that fails to draw the faithful into the mystery of redemption—either by introducing distracting elements into the text, or by using language which plays to the American bias for self-actualization rather than the liturgy's insistence on the reliance of all on the mercy of God—is a failure, despite its otherwise worthy character as public proclamation.

Translated Texts Respect the Narrative Form of Liturgical Prayer—Next, Campbell turns to an essential element of the form of many liturgical prayers: their "narrative quality." How is this sometimes elusive component to be defined? Campbell provides us with a succinct description: "By narrative form I mean a linguistic structure in which a story is told or elements of a story are related." Always concise, Campbell goes on to locate the key language feature of such narrative form: "This form is especially conducive to encountering the transcendent God, to strengthening the bond of union between them and their Lord, and to uniting them among themselves in Christ because the story is told 'in the language of "you" and "we."'" In other words by the use of the first- and second-person pronouns in the narration, those of us who hear the story realize our involvement in it. God's story and our story merge."

Campbell raises a subsequent issue: in the translation of the Roman Missal, how well and how often are the passages regarding the *mirabilia Dei* or wondrous acts of God—passages that form the basis of the Church's petition for help, and that are always in the Latin text structured in a narrative form—left in narrative English equivalents? Campbell briefly reviews how previous ICEL attempts to capture this important feature have been the occasion of criticism, but he commends ICEL's newer efforts at developing "'an openness to use a more complex English syntax' presupposing 'respect for the needs of proclamation.'"

Translated Texts Are Appropriately Metaphoric—Metaphor, Campbell maintains, is prevalent throughout the liturgy both in its ritual acts and in its language. To engage in liturgy, he writes, is to be engaged by metaphor. His point is directly made in relation to the translation of liturgical texts: "in the translation of Latin liturgical texts where metaphoric language occurs in the original, it should be preserved in some way in the translation—but also, where untraditional and overly-precise language is used in the Latin, a translator would be doing a service to render it more metaphorically in English."

Campbell illustrates this point by commenting on the need to preserve metaphoric images in the Eucharistic Prayers that describe not only what is visible to the faithful on the altar, but as well, what the visible elements stand for. Liturgical language, Campbell argues, makes use of metaphor instinctively, thereby calling into question any too-precise translation of phrases intentionally laden with a metaphoric sense. No matter what the clarifying or didactic intention, he concludes, of those who would "literalize" the metaphoric, a danger of impoverishing or even robbing liturgical language of its ability to engage the faithful in a new relationship with God and each other is always present in poorly conceived translation.

Translated Texts Incorporate Inclusive Language—Inclusive language, according to Campbell, is an important feature of liturgical translation that can help to promote the ideal kind of participation mentioned earlier in his paper: "the full, conscious and active" participation envisioned in *Sacrosanctum Concilium*, no. 14. He notes that while the use of "horizontal inclusivity" did not result in any Vatican objection during recent revisions in the publication of the expected *Lectionary for Mass*, nevertheless the use of "vertical inclusivity" has. Campbell then offers two reflections on this problem.

First, widespread, popularly used rewordings of certain responsories at Mass—for example, the *Suscipiat* or even the Preface dialogue—in which the masculine gender normally attributed to God through personal pronouns is discreetly substituted by non-gendered language seem to indicate that the faithful who find it difficult to pray always using exclusively masculine imagery for God also find such language inadequate. Campbell asks, "Does not, however, the locally widespread phenomenon of substitution for and elimination of masculine imagery for God in liturgical texts suggest that some of the language employed in these texts may be, at least, inadequate?" He notes, nevertheless, that two further dangers are evinced in this kind of substitutionism: (1) metaphoric language suffers or is eliminated from the text and (2) God is then spoken of using what Campbell calls "an inherently non-personal term to address the personal God."

Second, Campbell calls for a wider use of vertical inclusivity in liturgical language in order to "allow for more diverse, less limiting images of God." Again, he argues that only by doing so can more of the faithful relate more fully to and consistently engage in the divine mysteries being celebrated. Is this not, he concludes, the goal of all liturgical speech and act—to promote the full, conscious, and active participation that the Council so urgently recommends?

Translated Texts Are Substantial Enough for Repeated Use as Prayer over a Lengthy Period of Time—Campbell then turns his attention to an important quality of liturgical translation that, he writes, allows the faithful "ever greater access to the inexhaustible mystery celebrated in the liturgy," viz., depth of expression. He warns that euchological texts must be "rich enough to yield new insights" with each use. If texts are "too 'thin'" and surrender all their meaning at once, then repeated use will be impossible, while access to the mystery so described would be "difficult if not denied altogether." He goes on to give several illustrations of this point from the opening collects of the Roman Missal.

Linking his insight on depth of expression to the needs of the faithful more generally, Campbell remarks that the 1993 and

1997 ICEL translation styles show evidence of a corollary principle to the one just given: namely, that liturgical language that has depth and hence repeatability must also be taken from a more elevated or formal style of speech. He warns that a too-close following of the ideas in the 1969 instruction *Comme le prévoit*, which advocated "common usage" in liturgical language, could run the risk of diminishing the ability of the faithful to participate in a deep and repeatedly engaging way. Almost ironically, Campbell writes that it is the richness and fullness of liturgical texts that make a final quality of liturgical language possible: the quality of familiarity. When the faithful are familiar—i.e., have a sense of closeness or intimacy between the text prayed and the faith and affections that it is meant to form within the individual believer—then participation of a very high quality is possible.

A final reflection allied with this general point concludes Campbell's fifth section: that translators have a responsibility to "shape texts for *proclamation* in the liturgical assembly." In addition to concerns he articulated about vocabulary and syntax, the non-verbal elements of "rhythm, balance, and the like as part of the setting in which liturgical texts are proclaimed are *important*, then, for the transmission of their meaning."

***Translated Texts Respect the Principle of Organic Growth*—** Here, Campbell poses a question that has shaped much of the recent discussion on the translation of existing texts in the Roman Missal and the composition of new texts as suggested in *Sacrosanctum Concilium*: Is there a style of translation, either "dynamic equivalency" or "formal equivalency" (literal style), that better corresponds to the conciliar mandate that even the vernacularization of the liturgy "should in some way grow organically from forms already existing" (*Sacrosanctum Concilium*, no. 23)? For if either translated or newly composed texts are not directed by this principle of "organic growth," then, as Campbell writes, "organic growth is jeopardized." He is convinced that "organic growth is pastorally important because liturgy as ritual gives symbolic expression to what is at the heart of the communal life of the Church, becoming the principal vehicle for the transmission of the Church's tradition." And that tradition, in the end, must be consistently handed on from one generation of believers to the next, lest it be lost, and with it the means of accessing the divine mysteries that lies at the heart of a community's faith life.

Both sides of the issue have weighed in. Campbell notes that the formal equivalency side maintains, somewhat rigidly, that "as much of the detail in the Latin originals, including the form of the texts, [should] be preserved lest any of the meaning be lost and the faithful be deprived of their rightful inheritance." For such a position, contents exist *solely* in form.

The opposite position, "dynamic equivalency," maintains that in the spirit of *Comme le prévoit*, texts should be rendered in the vernacular more simply and straightforwardly, dispensing with Latin form wherever it fails to serve meaning and beauty in the vernacular. Campbell then asks whether both positions could not embrace the principle of organic growth to some extent. Indeed, he concludes, the choice of which style of translation is used should be made "on a case-by-case basis," with the translator opting for whichever presents the original texts in a way that allows hearers better, more direct access to their meaning.

Campbell's final remark is a call for the development of liturgical language that fulfills both its anthropological and transcendental goals. Again he cites the words of Don Saliers, stating that liturgical language "must delight and move and, above all, have a capacity to form and to express the deepest affections and virtues belonging to the word and mystery of God's self-communication."

Synthesis and Divergence Amongst the Presenters

Perhaps it was the final session of the Forum that seemed to allow some of the most creative exchanges of the two-day session. With each of the three presenters having read their impressive papers, and with every Forum participant (and observer) able to raise for each of the presenters numerous challenging issues on the nature of liturgical language and translation, attention at last could be drawn to asking follow-up questions: How do these seemingly differing positions support each other? Are there major areas of agreement between all the positions expressed that could, with time, become the basis of a common ground for understanding liturgical language and translation? And what account is to be made of the disagreements voiced here? Can they be resolved in a forum similar to what we had experienced over the last two days?

Towards the end of the second-to-last session, a tentative effort was made by the moderator to direct the general discussion towards a consideration of the common themes that appeared to run through all of the talks, and to ask the question of whether, in fact, many of the principal points were not complementary to each other—though, often enough, worded differently and offered from very diverse viewpoints. Below is first a general synthesis in which the essential elements of each presenter's thesis are juxtaposed so as to form what synthesis in their thinking may be possible within so complex a field. Second, an overview is offered on the central point of disagreement between two of the speakers, Ostdiek and Driscoll, whose views on textuality—which form so much of their translation philosophy—can be seen in contrast.

Complementarity in Viewpoints: A Possible Synthesis?
It should be stated again at the outset of this part of our discussion that each of the presenter's papers represented well their given points of view; each knew "his turf," as it were, whether in the relationship of linguistics and linguistic anthropology to liturgical science (Ostdiek), or the way in which patristic theology and rhetorical form help to fashion

Roman prayers (Driscoll), or the way in which pastoral issues of contemporary believers must inform the final translation of liturgical texts (Campbell). There is no doubting the competence and clear expression of each scholar.

What can be added is that, in a general way, there were essentially two important *methodological* positions advanced and one *pastoral* position, each with their own theological underpinnings. For Ostdiek and Driscoll, the debate turned to questions of method appropriate for the understanding and rendering of texts. For Campbell, however, the focus was less on method and more on the effects that well-rendered texts—however they are produced—should have on the believers who use them. Campbell styled himself as "neither a Latinist nor one engaged in the provision of texts for the liturgy, but as one who participates in liturgy daily" and who wished to address "some issues in the English translation of Latin liturgical texts as these pertain to the needs of participants in the liturgical act. . . ." His contribution to the Forum was, broadly put, to demand that all translation be answerable to the most obvious and final purpose of such texts: the worship they enable at the celebration of the Eucharist. From some six points of view, Campbell went on to explore every significant aspect of text-and-participation, from inclusive language to repeatability of use, to "full and active engagement" by the assembly which speaks or hears them. In a sense, Campbell offered a pastoral critique of both the methodological approaches, while deferring to those with expertise in language and historico-critical analysis on how such methods should be employed. It is a first point of synthesis to suggest that both Ostdiek's and Driscoll's work could be read critically from Campbell's viewpoint with great benefit.

Ostdiek brought to the Forum an immense competence in liturgical science, particularly as it has been studied since the Second Vatican Council through the lens of behavioral sciences. How many times, for example, did he offer his reader perspectives from anthropology, linguistics, psychology, semiotics, and many other relatively new disciplines that liturgical theology has embraced with enthusiasm? To the education of every reader, Ostdiek drew a new and breathtaking landscape that invited reconsideration of liturgical act and word over previous, more conventional perspectives. His contribution to the Forum was to emphasize how the "performative" aspects of prayer—and therefore, of translation—are surely the most noticeable to the faithful, forming believers by aesthetic sound and sure faith, thereby leaving them with "memory traces" that bind the worshipers with text and rite.

Driscoll's extended discussion was a compelling exposition of many aspects of textual preparation and exegesis, integrated, it would seem, through an application of monastic *lectio* as theological method. This in itself makes Driscoll's contribution both unique and highly valuable. His attention to detail in reconstructing patristic and historical nuance is unmatched in present commentary on the liturgy. Driscoll alerted his reader, at the start of his essay, that he would approach the translation of the Missal as a professional who renders "patristic texts into English." Driscoll's textual analysis—his scope and sequencing of elements to be ferreted out in the web of ancient compositional style that typifies Roman Missal texts—is a mastery that few can match. But one should note carefully that Driscoll's concentration is on the preparation of text for translation—i.e., his method produces a text that is then to be readied for the "performative" aspects of translation in which Ostdiek and others specialize. Driscoll's method, in a word, addresses questions that Ostdiek would generally consider *a priori* to his concerns. A second point of synthesis suggests, then, that the two methods of translation presented by Ostdiek and Driscoll could both be used beneficially by the liturgical translator—the one (Driscoll's) helping to map out a territory of historico-critical method to establish an ur-text in translation, which would then be fit for shaping by the other method (Ostdiek's), whose insights into performative detail could help to transform solid textual content into publicly proclamable prayer.

But apart from the use of select elements from both methods, it remains important to ask whether these two methods *in toto*, as presented by Ostdiek and Driscoll, are conceptually compatible for developing a synthetic approach to liturgical translation. We turn our attention now to a brief examination of a central point of divergence between the two, in order to clarify further the contribution of each.

A Point of Divergence: Whether the Meaning of a Roman Missal Text Can Be Accurately Apprehended

Each of the three presenters explored what current literary criticism means by the term "textuality,"—i.e., the qualities of effective written communication such as coherence, context, authorial intention, and the situation of the listener. In Driscoll's paper, this idea can be detected repeatedly in phrases such as "the inner voice of the text," "an understanding of the text in its own language," and his demand that a "liturgical vernacular" be developed as a part of realizing the conciliar vision for the reform of the liturgy. Within Ostdiek's thinking, various aspects of textuality were usefully explored under terms such as "texts in context" and the "narrative quality" of liturgical texts. Campbell's presentation cited at least three dimensions of textuality: the preservation of metaphoric—or poetic—language as a principal means of worship; narrative form in prayer; and the need to ensure the "organic development" of translations from their originals.

While it is obvious that some of these ideas, such as the narrative quality of liturgical prayer, are commonly addressed by two or even all three presenters, other concerns about textuality also seem to divide them. Perhaps the most obvious difference is clear in the presentations of Ostdiek and Driscoll, who each spent a significant amount of time addressing textuality from two complementary but non-convergent viewpoints. For while both would agree that (in Driscoll's words) the prayer texts of the Roman Missal are "oral and proclaimed, not written and read," or that (in Ostdiek's phrase) such texts are primarily "oral/aural," nevertheless their approaches to the preparation of text for the process of translation are noticeably different.

In Driscoll's scheme, the recovery or retrieval efforts to "understand exactly" the intentionality, tone, vocabulary, theological syntax, and historical meanings are paramount. Driscoll would ascribe all of these tasks to the mastery of "con-text" in his overall schema of pre-translation responsibilities. In effect, the product of a translator depends directly on the quality of work done on the pre-translation issues already listed. Questions of the aesthetic rendering of the text, its pastoral effectiveness, oral/aural design, and the like—sometimes categorized as "performative issues"—are subordinate to concerns about the need for reading each text fully in light of the tradition it represents more or less successfully, and most importantly, in light of the intent of the author. For Driscoll, a translator deals in the end with two texts: the original in Latin, and the vernacular in English—a vernacular whose final expression may be completely modern but also wholly recognizable as a part of the ancient prayer from which it was developed.

For Ostdiek, while it is fair to say that "discerning the meaning to be brought forward in translating a Latin text requires locating it in its original context," there is little likelihood of an exact process of location for any text. Conceding that, in some cases, this work can produce very specific understandings—such as of the dating of opening prayer for the eighth Sunday in Ordinary Time to the winter of A.D. 537-38—generally, Ostdiek cites the complexities of the composition process as a whole that would seem to work against such a retrieval effort. He points out, for example, that very often prayer texts have "passed through the hands of redactors of different times and historical-cultural contexts. Furthermore, the Latin rite is also noted for its use of the 'mosaic' principle by which a compiler borrows ideas and phrases from many different sources and blends them into one new prayer." The result is that "the meaning of the prayer text is never found in a pure state, as though its essence could be extracted from its cultural embodiment(s)." Textual meaning is, therefore, layered or interlaid, nearly prohibitive of the kind of analysis advocated by Driscoll.

Ostdiek is then poised to ask a central epistemological and textual question: "Which stage of meaning is to be taken as the authentic one?" His answer is practical in nature, rather than theological: "In such semantically complex and culturally multiple fields of discourse," he writes, "editorial choices have to be made." Ostdiek acknowledges that his approach "runs the risk, however, of fixing the meaning too precisely or narrowly, with the possibility of 'serious loss' of some aspects of multivalent meaning found in the tradition." He concludes with a sentence that seems to define the key difference between his own and Driscoll's thinking in the area of contextuality: "The way forward, then, might be to enlarge our working understanding of the liturgy as constituting a vast repertoire of prayer texts which collectively, rather than individually, proclaims the fullness of the faith to us." In other words, the close examination of texts, as advocated by Driscoll, that would produce his "exact understanding" of meaning is, for Ostdiek, a near impossibility, given the complexity of the transmission and composition history of such texts. Ostdiek's position, then, is to read the Roman Missal for its spirit, themes, teachings, virtues, and prayers as a whole, and then to apply a derived understanding of its message to the translation and composition of prayers for the present moment. On this one point, at least, Driscoll's thinking stands in sharp contrast. Driscoll proposes a detailed method for the retrieval and apprehension of meaning in ancient Roman Missal texts, a method that, essentially, Ostdiek's reflections call into doubt.

The consequences of each of these positions for liturgical translation are immense. For Driscoll, the quality of the translation is directly dependent upon the "exact meaning" of a prayer text, which is discoverable through a carefully drawn method of textual analysis. As a result, vernacularization can hope to identify and carry over multiple elements of the polyvalent sense of nearly every text, creating a detailed "road map," as it were, of the prayer's structure, form, syntax, intention, theology, and even its history. For Driscoll, an English rendering of Latin originals, which are made to disclose their secrets in this fashion, can maintain a very high correspondence between the two texts, while respecting the unique expressiveness of both languages.

For Ostdiek, such a process is fundamentally in question due to the likelihood that deconstructive methods can not accurately identify the multiple elements that constitute ancient texts such as those in the Roman Missal. Hence, Ostdiek writes, textual meaning can never be found in a "pure state, as though its essence could be extracted from its cultural embodiments." He writes that the blended texts of the Roman Missal have undergone processes of "successive transformations" that can result in finding in them "new enrichment and fresh vitality." Underlying these notions is the implicit central tenet of the theory of dynamic equivalency that Ostdiek has embraced: that form and meaning in an ancient composition can be separated from each other, and that, by implication, the meaning of such a text can then be reduced to propositions and the relationships between them. It is at this point in the translation process that Ostdiek calls for "editorial choices" that decide which level, which stage of meaning discerned from a given text is to be taken as authentic. Once determined, this meaning is then re-presented in new or equivalent forms from the receptor language.

Conclusion

The principal goal of the redesigned Forum on Translation was a simple one: to explore various viewpoints on the theory and practice of liturgical translation. Many diverse perspectives—from both the presenters and the participants—

emerged in papers and discussions. Clarity on the main lines of debate regarding translation from formal- and dynamic-equivalency perspectives were found; methods for applying each theory were outlined; and clear examples of how each theory functions in producing widely differing translations were discussed. It remains the task of ongoing scholarship to ask how both of these forms, in their continued development, can be brought to serve the conciliar vision of a renewed liturgy whose vernacular texts can promote a "full, conscious and active participation" (*Sacrosanctum Concilium*, no. 14) that is of such "great advantage to the people" (*Sacrosanctum Concilium*, no. 35).

NOTES

NOTES

NOTES

NOTES

NOTES

NOTES